History of France

Leon Amiel Publisher
New York

Concise History of Great Nations
General Editor: Otto Zierer

Jacques Levron France

Contents

1 From pre-history to the Merovingians 7
2 Merovingians and Carolingians 14
3 The Capetians 23
4 The Valois and the Hundred Years' War 33
5 Wars with Italy, Wars of Religion, the Renaissance 46
6 Henry IV and Louis XIII 54
7 The Sun-King 61
8 The Age of Enlightenment 69
9 The Revolution and the Empire 78
10 The Age of Revolutions 93
11 From defeat to victory 102
12 The contemporary period 114

Translation by David Macrae

Cover: King Louis II, Duke of Anjou, at the age of nine, being received at the gates of Paris by the Dukes of Berry and Burgundy (1386).
Title page: the Château of Versailles.

Credits:
Bibliothèque Nationale Paris – jacket. Fotogram – 4/5. Giraudon –
8, 10, 12, 13, 17, 23, 24, 28, 29, 30, 36, 37, 41, 45, 47, 48, 49, 52, 53, 55, 56,
57, 58, 59, 60, 61, 63, 64, 65, 68, 69, 70, 72, 73, 76, 77, 79, 80, 81, 84, 89,
93, 96, 100, 101, 102, 104, 107, 112. Media – 11, 16, 19, 31, 34, 35, 38, 39, 40,
42, 43, 50, 54, 66, 76, 78, 82, 86, 87, 90, 91, 94, 95, 97, 99, 101, 106, 110,
122, 123. Minerva – 47, 62, 89, 92, 98, 105. Viollet – 11, 15, 21, 26, 27, 33,
39, 44, 51, 56, 71, 74, 85, 103, 108, 111, 112, 114, 115, 116, 117, 118, 120, 121,
122.

Published 1977 by Leon Amiel Publisher
31 West 46th Street,
New York, N.Y. 10036,
U.S.A.

Library of Congress Catalog Card No. 77-73080
I.S.B.N. No. 0-8148-0672-4

© Media Books S. A., Nyon, 1976
Printed in Germany by Mohndruck Reinhard Mohn OHG, Gütersloh

1 From pre-history to the Merovingians

France is a very old country, having been inhabited as far back as pre-historic times. *Homo sapiens*—man with an erect posture, distinct from the animals—made his first appearance in this country, situated at the west-ernmost extremity of Europe, more than 15,000 years before the birth of Christ. He probably lived in caves, but was already capable of representing on the walls of those caves the image of the animals with which he was in everyday contact: the frescoes of the caves at Lascaux, and of other caves in the south-west, are evidence of a very mature taste and of some rather im-pressive artistic research.

The entire country which was later to become Gaul was already in-habited. Men put up enormous stones, called *menhirs* or *dolmens*, in honor of their gods or their dead. The extraordinary alinements to be found at Carnac, in Brittany, might be simp-ly burial grounds for their dead, but, whatever their original purpose, a great deal of patience and skill must have gone into the construction of these megaliths.

Dolmens, menhirs and stone tables occur over a wide area. The age of stone and of carved silex was followed by that of iron and then of bronze: man had learnt to use fire, with which he was able to make pottery and bronze statuettes. The *Venus of Les-pugue*, while not particularly beau-tiful, is one of the most ancient artistic renderings of woman, symbolizing fertility, the source of life and of all good things.

Century after century went by. During the first millenium before the birth of Christ, the Celts came out of Central Europe and invaded Gaul, mingling with the peoples they found already settled there, and bringing with them their own civilization.

Other ethnic groups also settled in Gaul: in Aquitaine, there was inter-marriage between the Celts and the Iberians, while, in the South East, the Celts mixed with the Ligurians.

To begin with, the Gauls—to call them by the name which Caesar used to designate them—were rather un-stable, and preferred livestock to crops. But they gradually began to merge into groups, drawn by the wealth of the soil and the prospect of improved trade. The discovery of the *Treasury of Vix*, (Côte-d'Or) from the 5th century BC, has made it clear that Gaul was already serving as an inter-mediary for trade between the Orient and Germany.

In the 6th century BC, the Greeks founded the colony of Massilia (Mar-seille) and spread out all around the Mediterranean. Nevertheless, they had to contend with the neighboring tribes of Celts and Ligurians, who were still largely uncivilized; yet Greek influence was to make itself felt in many ways, even providing a model for the design of Gaulish coins.

In the year 125 BC, the Romans intervened, on the request of Massilia, and soon extended their rule as far as Durance and Languedoc. However, in the rest of the country, the tribes which had assembled inside the forti-fied towns known as *oppida* had to fight the Cimbrians and the Teutons. The Sequans sent for help to Ario-vista, king of the Suevi. The ensuing profound divisions in Gaul were what caused Caesar to intervene.

Gaulish civilization

It would be unfair to regard the Gauls as primitive. Their civilization was essentially rural in nature: they opened up land for cultivation; their towns were small; their inhabitants were skilled at making weapons out of iron. They were a religious people, worshipping natural divinities, such as springs, trees. They used to offer sac-rifices to *Esus*, the god of war, or *Epona*, the goddess of sacrifices, who was represented as being on horse-back. Their priests, the Druids, used to assemble the faithful in the forests, to celebrate the festival of the mistle-toe. It should also be noted that the Gauls believed in the immortality of the soul.

The original forests in which these people lived still cover vast areas. The Gauls' dwellings were very simple round huts, in the middle of which there was a fireplace. Each tribe had its capital, situated, as in the case of Lutèce, Lyon, and Autun, at a river crossing, or on the top of a hill. The warlike, quarrelsome Gauls spent much of their time fighting other tribes; they were thought to fear only one thing—that the sky might fall on them. The rivalry between the various tribes greatly facilitated the conquest of Gaul by Julius Caesar.

The war in Gaul

In the year 58 BC, the Gaulish tribe of the Edueni appealed to the procon-sul Julius Caesar, who had just be-come established in Provence (Pro-vincia), to intervene so as to prevent the Helveti from settling on the ocean coast. Caesar drove the Helveti back to their point of departure and, later in the same year, forced Ariovistus to retreat to Germany. His legions took up winter quarters in Gaul, thereby annoying the Belgi (a Gaulish tribe between the Seine and the Rhine). In 57, Caesar defeated them on the Seille (or the Sambre), and, in 56, he attacked the Veneti, an Armorican people whose fleet, stationed in the Gulf of Morbihan, put up a brave struggle, before finally capitulating;

7

meanwhile, one of Caesar's lieutenants, Publius Crassius, subdued Aquitaine, from the Pyrenees to the Loire.

The fighting among the Gaulish chieftains was a distinct advantage to Caesar—for a while. In 52 BC, a young Gaulish chieftain leading the tribe of the Arverni realized the need to unite against Caesar and his legions. Vercingetorix was quite successful, to start with, as the Roman leader was not expecting such a general uprising. The Romans were beaten at Gergovia, where they had to lift the siege; however, showing great military skill, he exhausted the Gauls by compelling them to undertake numerous forced marches, and eventually drove them back to Alesia (probably Alise-Sainte-Reine, near Dijon). Some of the Gaulish tribes did not dare stand up to Caesar, and were simply tired of this endless war. After a heroic resistance, Vercingetorix finally surrendered, in order to save the lives of his men and the inhabitants of the *oppidum*. He was to remain a prisoner in Rome for six years, before watching, as one of the vanquished, the triumph of Caesar, and later being executed. Caesar had taken eight years to conquer the Gauls and push back the frontiers of the Roman Empire as far as the *limes germanicus* (the Germanic frontier).

Gallo-Roman civilization

What is known as the Gallo-Roman civilization then gradually came to be formed in the area: it was to last nearly three centuries and bring real peace to Gaul. The Gaulish tribes and the Romans took quite a long time to merge, however.

The ruins of the camps in which the Romans settled have been given the misleading name of *Caesar's camps*.

Actually, they were rest camps where the troops passed the winter; they were equipped with arenas and temples for their gods. In many cases, these camps were situated close to the towns.

The Gallo-Roman towns developed harmoniously. As there was no shortage of space, they spread out in all directions. The ruins of the monuments of this period are still to be found in numerous places, particularly in the South of France: the *maison carrée* at Nîmes, gates (Autun), triumphal archways, arenas with seating capacity for several thousand spectators. Their houses were comfortable, most of them having baths and geo-thermal heat, as thermal springs provided hot, warm and cold water. Most houses had an *atrium*, or inner courtyard, while the rooms were often paved with fine decorative mosaics.

The towns also contained temples to the Roman gods, though the Gauls, particularly in rural areas, remained faithful to druidic forms of worship. Farming seems to have been very well organized, with high yields; the principal house in a given domain—the *villa*—was comfortable, roomy and elegant.

In order to enable their legions to move easily from one province to another the Romans built a huge road network throughout Gaul, complete with bridges at river crossings—the most famous example being the Pont du Gard, built between 56 and 100 AD.

Administratively, Gaul was divided into provinces: the First and Second Lyon, first and Second Aquitaine, Narbonne, Belgium, etc. The city, or *civitas*, continued to be the unit of territorial administration, though its size varied greatly. Most commonly, the

former capital of the Celtic tribes became the new provincial capital, often taking the name of Julius Caesar: *Caesarodunum, Augustodunum*, etc. Lutèce was already a major city, being the headquarters of the Parisii. Many of its fine monuments were built by Emperor Julian the Apostate, who lived there frequently from 331 to 363.

The large landowners were able to draw on an abundant supply of farm labor, based on the social system practised in Rome. There were numerous slaves or serfs (*servi*). However, peasant revolts did occur from time to time, particularly between 269 and 284.

Gaul becomes evangelized

Christianity made its first appearance in southern Gaul towards the end of the 1st century, but it was not until the middle of the 2nd century that the first saints and martyrs, such as Pothin in Lyon or Denis in Paris, founded Christian communities. Most of the saints who preached the Gospel were persecuted by the Roman emperors and martyrized; they included many women such as St. Blandine, who showed great courage in the face of death.

The spread of Christianity in Gaul was a slow process: it took more than three centuries for the Gauls to abandon their old tutelary gods. In rural areas, the peasants remained faithful to the traditional forms of worship, which explains why *peasant* is synonymous with *pagan* (paganus).

Hilary of Poitiers and St. Martin were the great apostles of the Gauls. St. Martin was bishop of Tours, and fought paganism vigorously until his death in 397. More than 4,000 parishes in France are dedicated to him, and he still has numerous disciples.

9

This impressive rooster, with its splendid tail and proud bearing, is from the Celtic period. The rooster was the emblem of the Gauls, and is still, in modern times, one of the symbols of France.

Bishoprics were founded gradually, in most cases in the main community of each *civitas*. The great landowners built chapels for those who worked in their service and for the artisans or craftsmen who lived on their estate. This chapel then became the parish church. This is the origin of many villages which bear the landowner's name: Savigny, residence of Savin, Flavigny, residence of Flavian, etc.

The first invasions

Under Roman rule, Gaul became a rich, fertile land, and, as such, naturally attracted the envious attention of tribes from beyond the Rhine. About the year 275, the Germans first crossed the *limes germanicus*, the frontier which separated them from the Roman Empire. At first, these raids were on a rather small scale, yet,

even so, they succeeded in frightening the local population. As a means of protection, most of the cities then built thick fortifications, many of which still stand. The enclosure formed by these Gallo-Roman structures was somewhat cramped, but had to accommodate the governor's palace, the bishop's palace, the cathedral, and a number of streets for tradesmen and craftsmen. Today, one can form some idea of the small size of these communities, which had anywhere between 5,000 and 15,000 inhabitants (Marseille). To their best of their ability, the Gauls defended themselves against the invaders. This period was to last a whole century.

The great invasions

The year 410 marked the beginning of a succession of invasions. Some

tribes, like the Suevi, Sarmati and the Alani, were content to cross the country without settling in it: the Alani passed through leaving the first name Alain as the only evidence of their presence in Gaul, while the Sarmati gave their name to a number of communities (Sermaise). However, some tribes settled in various parts of Gaul, bringing with them their laws and religions, which were not those practised in Rome . . . The Visigoths, who followed the heresy of Arius, settled in the south-west of Gaul and the area which was later to be known as Languedoc. The Burgondes moved into the east of Gaul (modern Burgundy and Provence). The Vandali crossed Gaul without stopping.

The Roman Empire was now clearly on the point of collapse. The last emperors delegated their authority to chieftains who did what they could to exercise it, with the aid of mercenary soldiers. For example, a Gallo-Roman chief, Aetius, successfully fought off the invasion of the Huns; he secured the assistance of the Visigoths, the Burgondes and a tribe which had settled in north and northern and eastern Gaul: the Franks.

One cannot be really sure about the precise nature of these invasions; sometimes they were peaceful, as the Gallo-Romans preferred to share their land with the invaders; others were quite brutal and caused widespread destruction. Many Gallo-Roman estates were burned to the ground. The cities held out far better, as Attila saw for himself when he tried to invade Gaul in the mid-5th century.

The Huns

The Huns, who were originally from Asia and had settled in Central Europe, were neither more primitive

The minting of coins is one of the signs of authority. In the time of Vercingetorix, the Gauls were already striking their own coins, many of which have been discovered during excavations. Shortly thereafter, however, Julius Caesar was to conquer Gaul, though his task was made difficult by the sustained resistance of certain Celtic tribes. After his final victory, Gaul entered upon a long period of peace.

nor more cruel than most of the other invaders. Yet they had a reputation for cruelty which certain historical expressions—probably unfounded—have sustained right up to the present day.

They were certainly avid conquerors. Under their leader Attila, they invaded Gaul in 451, captured and destroyed Metz, and laid siege to Lutèce. The panic-stricken inhabitants of the city were seriously thinking of surrender, when a simple shepherdess named Geneviève, later canonised by the Church, put the men to shame, and restored the defenders' courage. Attila abandoned his attempt to take Lutèce by siege and turned instead, to Orleans. However, Bishop Aignan, leading the defense of the city, held out until the arrival of a relief army, whereupon Attila withdrew to the east. He tried in vain to take Troyes, in the face of stubborn resistance from Bishop Saint Loup. The leader of the Gallo-Romans, Aetius, with the help of the Visigoths, the Burgondes and the Franks, struck at the invader near Troyes, most probably at Moirey, and defeated his armies convincingly, in the battle of the Catalaunian Fields. The hordes of the Huns retreated and left Gaul altogether.

The appearance of the Franks

The Franks of Merovea were among the tribes which fought against Attila. They were Germans who had settled, in the early 5th century, in the north and north-west of Gaul. The Franks consisted of several tribes; the Salian Franks, whose capital was at Tournai, and the Ripuarian Franks, who were so named because they had settled along the banks of the Rhine. This warlike, courageous people acclaimed as king a man whom they lifted up on a shield Their laws were

These miniatures depict scenes from the Merovingian period. The baptism of Clovis by St. Remi was an event of major significance. The Franks continued to be barbarians, as can be seen from the crimes of Frede-gonde, who is here shown next to Chilperic. King Dagobert (lower right) was renowned for his wisdom.

still somewhat barbarous, though, on the whole, they were far from being primitive in their ways. Their weapons were often chiselled, and their women had jewelry; they were skilful, industrious and hard-working.

Is it safe to say that the first known Frankish king was Pharamond? Many people think that, like Chlodion, he existed only in legend. However, Merovea, who gave his name to the dynasty, did actually reign, most probably from 448 to 457 or 458. The Frankish conquest was to begin during the reign of his son, Childeric.

Gaul in the middle of the 5th century

Gaul was occupied almost exclusively by peoples which had invaded it; the Franks held the left bank of the Rhine and Belgium. The Armoricans, who had withstood Roman influence much better, were invaded by the Bretons, who had come over from the British Isles. Occupation varied from peaceful to violent. The Visigoths occupied large areas in the center, west and south-west, from the Loire to the Pyrenees. The Basques lived on two slopes of the Pyrenees, and the Burgondes lived to the west.

In theory, these peoples were part of the Roman Empire, with a sort of federal status. However, the Empire disappeared in 476. After Aetius, two Gallo-Roman chiefs were to maintain the fiction of Roman rule: Aegidius and his son Syagrius. Their rule extended from the Seine to the Loire.

Whereas the Gallo-Romans continued to be governed by Roman law, the invaders had their own laws, customs and religions; most of them were Arians, in the sense that they professed the heresy of Arius, which had been condemned by the Roman Church, while the Gallo-Romans were faithful to Rome.

2 Merovingians and Carolingians

Childeric, the king of the Salian Franks, who had acceded to the throne in 458, was initially allied to the chief of the Romans, Aegidius, whom he helped to defeat the Visigoths near Orleans in 460. Six years later, he came to the aid of the Roman Count Paul, and, with him, drove out the Saxons who had occupied a part of Brittany. After the collapse of the Roman Empire, Syagrius, the son of Aegidius, chose to name himself King of the Romans. He stayed on good terms with Childeric, who died in 480, and was buried at Tournai, his capital city.

Clovis

Childeric's son Clovis was only fifteen years of age when he was made king. He was a tough, energetic adolescent, whose first aim was to put an end to the self-styled "King of the Romans"; he attacked Syagrius in 486, forcing him to take refuge at Toulouse with Alaric, the king of the Visigoths. Clovis compelled Alaric to execute Syagrius, and then proceeded to extend his own kingdom as far as the Loire, the frontier of the Visigoth kingdom. Later, he turned his attention to the small Frankish kingdoms of his brothers or cousins, in northern Gaul, overthrew them and annexed their lands.

In 493, he married the niece of Gondebaud, king of the Burgondes; Clotilde was a Christian princess. Clovis, however, remained faithful to his gods, so Clotilde enlisted the aid of Remi, the Bishop of Reims, in an attempt to convert her husband.

In 496, at the request of the Ripuarian Franks, who were being threatened by the Alamans, Clovis attacked the raiders at Tolbiac (Zülpich, southwest of Cologne). During the battle, Clovis promised to convert to the God worshipped by his wife, if he were victorious. He eventually did win the battle, and, on 25 December, he was baptised, together with 3,000 of his warriors, by Bishop Remi, at Reims. This was turning-point in the history of Gaul: thitherto, the tribes which had occupied the country were largely pagan or Arian. By recognizing the Roman Catholic Church, Clovis secured the support of the bishops and the clergy.

Then, after fighting the powerful king of the Burgondes, Gondebaud, Clovis concluded an alliance with him, and, in 507, was able to turn his attention to Alaric who was the King of the Visigoths, and an Arian. The ensuing conflict had all the features of a real crusade. At the battle of Vouillé, near Poitiers, Clovis won a resounding victory: Alaric II was killed, and his son had to flee to the Ostrogoths, with the result that Clovis now held sway over the entire south-west and Languedoc. A year later, he made a vain attempt to conquer Provence, which had been seized by Theodoric. Nonetheless, the Byzantine Emperor Anastasias sent him the insignia of consul in 509, thus enabling Clovis to wear the purple mantle of that rank, much to his satisfaction. In 511, he assembled the first national council of the Bishops of Gaul, at Orleans. He died on the following 27 November.

On account of Clovis and his conquests, the Franks now held almost all of Gaul. Only Brittany (in any case an ally of theirs), Provence and Lesser Brittany were still not under their authority.

The successors to Clovis

The four sons of Clovis shared the territory of Gaul into four parts, like a cake, yet kept their capital cities quite close to each other: Thierry was king of Reims, Clodomir was king of Orleans, Childebert was king of Paris and Clotaire was king of Soissons. After an initial period in which they carried on their father's conquests, they soon began to quarrel among themselves. Eventually, a fortunate chain of events made it possible for Clotaire, who had received the smallest share, to assume the entire inheritance. He died in 561.

These Frankish kings were still thoroughly barbarous; for example, they did not hesitate to use assassination as a means of getting rid of a rival for power. This is particularly true of the sons of Clotaire. The long wars which ravaged Austrasia (eastern

The Battle of Poitiers. *It is thought that the famous battle took place at this spot. The landscape has changed greatly since the year 732. Nevertheless, Charles Martel's victory had far-reaching consequences, because the Franks' success in stopping the Arab invasion saved the Christian West from the Infidel.*

Gaul) and Neustria (western Gaul) were aggravated and sustained by the frightful rivalry between Fredegonde, a former serving-girl who had married King Childeric I, and Brunehaut, the widow of Sigebert. This protracted struggle, which lasted throughout the latter part of the 6th century, ended in 613, when Clotaire II ordered the execution of Brunehaut. A detailed account of those events has come down to us thanks to the writings of Gregory of Tours, who can truly be called the father of French historiography.

The Merovingian kings were surrounded by a court in which posts of responsibility were both public and private: the marshal was in charge of the stables and commanded the cavalry, while the seneschals (the oldest rank) administered justice on behalf of the king. The nobles who lived close to the king were consulted by him on important matters, but the main figure in the Merovingian court was the *major domus*. Since the holder of this rank had control over foodstuffs, his authority and power were so great that, as in the case of Ebroin, for example, they exceeded those of the king himself. The struggles between the *major domus* of Neustria and those of Austrasia were unending.

Dagobert

Gaul suffered greatly from internal strife. Dagobert (604–639) succeeded in eliminating his parents and unifying Gaul once more under his rule, while, at the same time, allowing the nobles of Austrasia, under Bishop Arnoul of Metz, and those of Aquitaine, a measure of independence. He tried to subdue Lesser Brittany, but failed in the attempt.

He was held in high esteem, as a wise and judicious king. He protected the Church, and promoted the growth of the economy by instituting trade fairs, such as the Lendit fair, at Saint-Denis. He gave generously to the Abbey of Saint Denis, and, with the aid

of his minister Eloi, bishop of Noyon and goldsmith of the kingdom, succeeded in imposing the royal will on the nobles and the *major domus.* Dagobert died on January 19, 639, and was buried at Saint-Denis.

Merovingian civilization and institutions

The Merovingians applied their own *Salic law* in Gaul; it consisted of a body of Germanic customs which had been only slightly influenced by Roman law. A noteworthy feature is the system of redemption, whereby, on payment of a specific amount, the *wehrgeld,* it was possible to avoid corporal punishment. The amount involved varied according to the gravity of the offense. Disputes were taken before a court known as the *mallus.*

The army was one of the organs of government. All free men were obliged to do military service. Twice a year, the king reviewed his troops in the field of March and the field of May. The story of the *vase of Soissons,* which had been seized as booty by a soldier whom Clovis subsequently killed as a punishment, means more than a mere act of vengeance by the chief—it shows that the Frankish king saw to it that men under arms observed a certain code of conduct.

Little remains now of the architecture of the Merovingians, though the excellence of their work with gold and silver is evident from samples which have been recovered. The discovery of the tomb of Queen Aregonda at Saint-Denis has given us a good idea of the sophisticated levels to which they had already taken their art.

The Church grew and monasteries were founded. Queen Radegonda, wife of Clotaire II, retired to a convent which she herself had founded at Poitiers. Literature was also cultivated at this time: the Bishop of Clermont, Sidoine Apollinaire, was quite a talented poet.

EXCELSA VO

The last of the Merovingians

The last Merovingian kings are usually thought of as being idle and unproductive. They are often shown stretched out comfortably on an ox-drawn chariot, followed by their wife, children, concubines and faithful supporters (or *trustis*), as they made their way from one estate to another.

While this traditional image is cer-

Charlemagne, the great emperor. In this miniature he is shown crowned and carrying the imperial scepter. The beard, of course, is strictly apocryphal, as Charlemagne was smooth-chinned throughout his life.

tainly not wholly inaccurate, it does need some additional explanation. The truth of the matter was that these weak, and usually young kings, worn out by lavish pleasures at an early age, really had to live in this way; when they found food in short supply on one of their estates, they had to take to the road and go on to another of their properties.

The nobles, or *viri inlustres*, spent much of the time squabbling among themselves; in both Neustria and Austrasia, they shifted their support from one king or potentate to another, thus causing all the wars which sapped the strength of Gaul precisely when it was being threatened by grave danger.

Charles Martel and the Arabs

The Arabs, or Saracens, having ravaged the Mediterranean coast and overrun Spain, tried to invade Gaul. At the beginning of the 8th century, Charles, son of Pippin II, had become the sole master of Gaul. He had triumphed over the Frisons and the Saxons, and had had himself recognized as lord of Neustria and Austrasia alike. After the Arabs reached Aquitaine, Charles fought and defeated them on October 17 732, near Poitiers, at the mouth of the Vienne and the Clain. The Arab leader Abd el-Rahman was killed, and the Christian cause triumphed; the Saracens withdrew from Gaul altogether, though they laid waste the country as they went.

The end of the dynasty

The successful outcome of the battle of Poitiers greatly enhanced Charles' reputation, and resulted in his assuming the nickname *Martel* (*marteau*, hammer), because he struck with such force. When he died, in 741,

Charles the Bald, the son of Emperor Louis the Pious, became the
first king of the Franks, after the Treaty of Verdun. This 10th-century
miniature shows a scene which recurred quite often: the king, surrounded by his advisers, is granting an audience to rebellious subjects
who have come to seek pardon. Charles spent years fighting disaffected
groups such as the Bretons and the Basques.

his son Pippin, who was known, in the 9th century, as Pippin the Short, on account of his small stature, came to power jointly with his brother Carloman. The two men got on well together, and removed their adversaries from the scene. However, there was still a Merovingian king on the throne, and he was entirely in the hands of the major influential figures known as the *major domus*. In November 751, Pippin, having secured the support of the bishops and the nobles, and the encouragement of Pope Zacharias, had himself elected king at Soissons. The last Merovingian king was shut up in a monastery. The dynasty was over.

Pippin the Short

Pippin had been elected by the nobles, and consecrated by Archbishop Boniface: here we have two features of the monarchy, in that it wished to have a popular base and, at the same time, to be the allied with the Church. In 754, Pope Stephen II went to Gaul in order to seek the aid of the king of the Franks against the Lombards; while he was there, he anointed Pippin's two sons, Charles and Carloman, thereby strengthening the new dynasty. In 755–756, the new King of the Franks fought the Lombards, subdued south-eastern Gaul (with Narbonne) and the forces of Aquitaine under Duke Waifre. After Pippin's death in 768, his two sons came to power, but Carloman withdrew into a monastery in 771, leaving Charles as the sole King of the Franks.

A great conqueror

Charles was of medium build, broad-shouldered and beardless (the emperor with the flowing beard is straight out of legend); at the same time, he was a good administrator, and a conqueror who spent the first thirty years of his reign fighting the Lombards, the Moslems of Spain and, above all, the Saxons. In response to an appeal from Pope Hadrian, Charles resumed his father's struggle against the Lombards, taking their king, Didier, prisoner at Pavia in 774. He then proclaimed himself King of the Lombards.

Each year, with the coming of the fine weather, the toughest campaigns took place against the Saxons, a pagan people from northern Germany. Despite their courage they were often defeated in battle, though they usually took up arms again as soon as the Frankish troops had withdrawn. Eventually, the chief of the Saxons, Widukind, surrendered, and, together with his followers, became converted to Christianity. Charles generously allowed him to remain at the head of his kingdom. He stopped at the Elbe, which, in his opinion, was the outermost limit of Christian Europe.

However, Charles did not fare so well in Spain; he organized several campaigns against the Moors, but without much success. It was on the way back from one such expedition in Spain that Roland was attacked in the passes of Roncevaux by the Vascones who had come down from their mountain retreats. Though this was a fairly simple incident, it happened to be immortalized by the poets of the XIIth century in the form of a *chanson de geste*, and became a genuine epic.

Charles longed to see Europe Christian and united. He was now the master of the whole of Gaul, except for Brittany, which had remained independent, a large part of Germany, of Italy and even of northern Spain. In an attempt to organize these heterogeneous peoples, he divided his domains into *comtés* (the notion of the county already existed under the Merovingians) headed by a *comte* (or count)—from the word *comes,* or companion, from the palace. The palace was truly the central organ, closest to the king, comprising the *ministeriales,* or highly-placed dignitaries, who advised him. In frontier areas, Charles established the dukes. The counts governed the *pagus,* or county, in coordination with the bishops (and, sometimes, in competition with them). Their job was to find manpower for the *ost,* or army, among the free men of the population. Charles kept a check on their administration by creating the *missi dominici,* or king's envoys, who inspected the counties, heard the complaints of the people, and administered justice as they went, thus performing a temporal and a moral role at the same time. The *missi dominici* went about in pairs—one bishop and one layman—a fact which further emphasized the moral nature of their duties.

In order to unify legislation, Charles drafted the Capitularies, which were so called because they were divided into chapters; they consisted of either instructions for the use of the *missi dominici,* or texts governing the administration of the various domains, or the status of land, as in the famous *Capitulaire de Villis.*

Though not an educated man himself, Charles established schools and saw to it that his future officials were themselves well educated. He reformed the script in use in his day, which had become illegible under the Merovingians. He was a very pious man, and helped his best advisers, such as Mincmar, archbishop of Reims, to reform monastic life, which had begun to suffer from a number of abuses. Economic prosperity re-

19

"From the fury of the Normans deliver us, oh Lord!" This invocation must have been in frequent use among the inhabitants of Lutèce, when the fearsome warriors from the north swept up the Seine and attacked the capital of the Frankish kingdom in 885. This 19th-century engraving shows the Normans, on their fast drakkars, laying siege to Paris.

turned. This was truly a Renaissance, the Carolingian Renaissance.

Emperor Charlemagne

The Church was naturally grateful to Charlemagne for all he had done on its behalf; so, as an expression of its thanks, Pope Leo III crowned him Emperor, on 25 December 800, to the acclaim of the multitude. Though he fully expected this to happen, Charles nonetheless feigned surprise. Now there were two empires: the old Byzantine Empire, headed by a woman, Empress Irene, and the Western Empire, which had just been born.

Between the years 800 and 806, Charles succeeded in pacifying Saxony and concluding the struggle against the Avars. Thenceforth, he was to divide his time between his capital at Aix-la-Chapelle and his other palaces; his life grew more and more sedentary, yet he still strove to keep a firm grip on his immense empire, made up of such a wide variety of ethnic groups. In 806, at Thionville, he divided his States among his three sons, Charles, Pippin and Louis. However, as Pippin became a monk and Charles died, Louis eventually inherited the empire and was proclaimed Emperor, on September 1, 813, by the nobles assembled at Aix. Charles the Great (*Karolus Magnus,* or Charlemagne) died in that same city in January 814.

Louis the Pious and his sons

Louis, who was consecrated as Emperor at Reims, in October 816, by Pope Stephen V, continued the work his father had started, though he was certainly a far less resolute character. His weakness, and the influence wielded over him by his second wife Judith, were to give rise to serious un-

rest in the empire. In 817, Louis had already divided up the empire among the three of his sons who had been born to his first wife; in that same year, he recognized Lothaire, his eldest son as Emperor, but the birth of Charles, who was his son by his second wife, opened up the whole question of the succession all over again. A bloody struggle ensued during which, at one point, Louis was even overthrown by his children, and later re-instated on the throne.

These quarrels could not fail to weaken the authority of the king, to the benefit of the nobles, who gradually dissociated themselves from his rule. A number of other grants of power made the discord even worse, and when Louis the Pious died, in 383, the fighting broke out again, this time worse than before. In 841, Charles and Louis united against Lothaire, won the battle of Fontenoy-en-Puisaye, and, in September 843, in the presence of their followers assembled at Strasbourg, they uttered the famous oaths which, for the first time, had been drafted in the vernacular tongue. Lothaire abandoned the struggle, and, in September 843, the three surviving brothers signed the Treaty of Verdun: Lothaire, with the title of Emperor, received the territories between the mouths of the Escaut and Italy; Charles received France, and Louis Germany.

The unity of Europe was broken. In the words of the poet Florus: "Alas! Instead of a king, we now have kinglets, and instead of a kingdom, we have pieces of kingdoms!"

The social classes under the Carolingians

As can be seen from the monuments of the period which have survived in both France and Germany, Carolingian civilization was brilliant. As for the structure of society, there were a number of social classes. First, there were the large land-owners, who, in many cases, could trace their origins back to Roman Gaul, and who entrusted their lands to serfs or settlers. Between, the serf and the free men—whose number was rising considerably, on account of the dangers facing those who were not pro-

20

tected—there were many distinct levels. Besides the large landowners, the Church owned vast properties from which it sought to derive the greatest possible benefit. The nobles owed the emperor (or the king) the service of *ost*. Bishops and abbots were represented by an advocate. Administration, justice and finance were all in the hands of the count (*comte*), who, as the dangers increased, gradually

became more and more independent of the royal authority.

The Norman invasions

Towards the end of the 8th century, invaders from the north (whence the name *Norman*) began to lay waste the coasts of Gaul. Charlemagne had organized some measure of resistance to their advance; but it was not until 841 that the invasion really struck into the

hinterland. Moving swiftly, on boats with a figure-head of a dragon (*drakkars*), they swept inland, up the rivers, destroying everything in their path. In the face of this pagan onslaught, the monks had to flee, taking with them the relics of their founding saints. In 866, Robert le Fort, Duke of the area between the Seine and the Loire, made a vain attempt to stop them at Brissarthe. He was defeated and killed. The whole of France lived in a state of mounting insecurity.

Things we would not have been so bad if the kings, at least, had been able to agree among themselves. Yet, in 858, Louis of Germany tried to invade France. A reconciliation took place two years later, on the death of Lothaire: Charles and Louis shared out his kingdom, Charles getting Besançon, Lyon, Vienne and Grenoble. The disappearance of Louis II, King of Italy and Emperor (he was Lothaire's eldest son), made the throne available. Pope John VIII chose Charles and crowned him in Rome on 25 December 875. However, for three quarters of a century, the power of the emperor had steadily declined. Charles the Bald died in 877.

The end of the Carolingians

Thereafter, the dynasty became weaker and weaker. Louis the Stammerer, Louis III and Carloman (all reigning together) made a vain attempt to stop the Norman fleet. In 879, the Duke of Boson carved out a kingdom for himself in the southeast of France. In 881, Louis III succeeded in defeating the Normans at Saucourt-en-Vineuil. When these two kings died, the nobles gave their preference to Charles the Fat, son of Louis the German. Charles lost interest in France, and when the Normans laid siege to Paris in 885, the city was defended by Eudes, son of the Robert the Strong. Charles decided, shamefully, to come to terms with the enemy; he had them leave on payment of a large sum of money, and, moreover, allowed them to plunder Burgundy. When Charles the Fat died in 888, Eudes governed until Charles the Simple came of age.

Charles, who assumed power in 898, also favored reaching some sort of accommodation with the Normans; in 911, at Saint-Clair-sur-Epte, he signed a treaty ceding to them a part of Neustria, which later became Normandy. At the time, the house descended from Robert the Strong was consolidating its power, the last Carolingian kings, Louis IV d'Outremer and Lothaire were quite powerless. In 978, Emperor Otto tried to take Paris, but without success. As a result, loyalty to the Carolingian kings was briefly strengthened. However, in 987, when Louis V died after falling from a horse, when he had been king for only one year, Hugues, son of Duke Hugues le Grand, had no difficulty getting himself elected King of France by the nobles assembled at Noyon, with the aid of Archbishop Adalbéron, as Louis V had died childless.

Such was the pitiful end of a dynasty which, under Charlemagne and even for a while during the reign of Louis the Pious, had known great glory. The collapse of central authority and the weakening of the power of the king led to the formation of the feudal system.

These pictures, which are based on the seals of the first two Capetian kings, represent Hugues Capet, 'by the mercy of God king of the Franks', and his son Louis the Pious. At that time, the Capetian kingdom was quite modest.

3 The Capetians

The feudal system

The feudal system, which emanated from the weakness of the last of the Carolingian kings, was characterized by some rather special relations between the members of society, and by the exchange of part of one's freedom for the promise of protection. For the sake of security, certain particularly powerful or energetic men seized power; then, having become masters of an area, they received the homage of their vassals, granting them, in return, certain land: the fiefs. Noble vassals, kneeling before their sovereign, paid homage (either simple or liege). They undertook to help him in certain cases, and to go to war with him for a given time. Non-noble vassals—the commoners, churls, etc., made a statement recognizing the sovereignty of his overlord, paid duties, in the form of tax and statutory labor, paid tolls for the upkeep of roads and bridges, and had to use the common oven or mill.

It was about this time that fortresses began to be built. Originally of wood, they came to be built of stone by the end of the 9th century. Within their sturdy walls, the vassals of each overlord felt themselves to be secure. The inhabitants of the towns belonged to the system by coming under a given church, bishopric, chapter of a cathedral or a lay overlord. In turn, the Church also belonged to the system, and had its own vassals. The advocate of the bishop or the abbey did homage to his overlord on behalf of his master. Each overlord was himself subordinate to another lord, at a higher level. The great *seigneuries* came into being in this way: Champagne, Burgundy, Provence, the *comtés* of Toulouse, Auvergne, the duchy of Aquitaine, the *comté* of Anjou, Brittany (which had been virtually independent under the Carolingians), duchy of Normandy, the *comtés* of Flanders, Hainaut, etc. The lords at the head of these seigneuries gave homage to the king. The feudal system thus formed a pyramid which reached from the humblest vassal up to the king, who gave homage only to God.

The two essential features of the régime were vassalhood and the granting of fiefs. While strengthening these bonds, the Capetians were to attempt to expand their own domain at the expense of the great seigneuries.

The first Capetians

The first Capetians were not a very impressive lot! The domain of Hugues Capet (so named because he used to wear a cope) covered the area around Paris, reaching as far as Orleans—about the size of *one* modern *département*. But Hugues was the lord, and even if he was challenged when he tried to intervene in a dispute between two lords ("Who made you a count? – Who made you king?"), he was recognized as far south as the Pyrenees. Moreover, he enjoyed the support of the Church, and had had the sense to have his son Robert crowned as early as 987. By associ-

23

es du souldan debabilome p͠o tuer par
venir le roy et les treigneur͠s de son off

Come cestui roy p͠mist le port de dammette iiij v͠ uj
ll derreiner vindrent les nefez
lles vaisseaulx que len ot allocce
et si vindrent plusieurs nefe
des ysles z les barons z les thenaliere
et les autres pellerins qui auoient de

This 15th-century miniature illustrates the story of the landing of the Crusaders in the Holy Land. The great upsurge of faith which inspired the Christian world late in the 11th century led to the creation of the Frankish kingdom of Jerusalem. The crusades were not motivated solely by religious feelings: they made it possible to develop trade with the East.

ating him with the throne in this way, he saw to it that the succession was virtually assured. And in 996, his son Robert, later to be known as the Pious, succeeded him with no trouble at all.

The gloom of the 11th century

About the year one thousand, people began to think that the end of the world was close at hand. In fact, the terrors of that year have been greatly exaggerated. France became covered, in the expression of one chronicler, with a "white mantle of churches". This was the age of Romanesque art, with its use of the semi-circular arch, its characteristic barrel-roof, thick, massive columns and small dim interiors. Its sculptures were both naive and beautiful. The spread of the monastic movement led to the construction of many new buildings.

The monarchy remained weak, and could do little to prevent the private wars which occurred frequently throughout the 11th century. The great barons fought among themselves, seeking to expand their domains, as was the case with a certain Fouques Nerra, count of Anjou, who fought equally well against the Bretons and the counts of Blois. Meanwhile the people as a whole suffered. The Church instituted the Holy Truce, meaning that fighting was prohibited during certain periods, and the right of asylum. The first Capetians intervened in order to subdue the lords of neighboring territories, though they were not uniformly successful.

Just at that moment, William the Bastard, Duke of Normandy, landed in England and became master of the country after the battle of Hastings (1066). The resulting situation presented the Conqueror with an unusual paradox: he was King of England, while, in Normandy, he was a vassal of the King of France. The perils of such a state of affairs were obvious.

The successors of Hugues Capet—Robert the Pious (996–1031), Henry I (1031–1060) and Philip I (1060–1108), who was excommunicated by the Church for adultery—disappeared without leaving much for history to remember them by. Nonetheless, the Capetian monarchy already enjoyed fairly good standing, as Henry I married a Russian princess, Anne of Kiev, thus marking the beginning of a long relationship between the two countries, and, moreover, because it was from France that the first Crusade set off, late in the 11th century, for the Holy Land.

The first Crusade

The Holy Land and Jerusalem had fallen into the hands of the infidels. Was Christianity simply going to sit by and do nothing? In response to Pope Urban II, who had come to France to consecrate a number of churches, thousands of men took up the cross. Although a first crusade of poor people assembled by Peter the Hermit failed to complete the long journey, the nobles led by Godefroi de Bouillon did reach Palestine, and, on July 15, 1099, took Jerusalem.

The Pope had promised absolution of sin and a number of moral and material advantages to all those who took up the cross. The movement which culminated in the conquest of the Holy Land was fed by an immense upsurge of faith and enthusiasm. In keeping with feudal custom, the barons divided up Palestine into kingdoms and principalities. In his humility, Godefroi de Bouillon was content to accept the title of Advocate of the Holy Sepulcher. The Order of the Templars, with the role of caring for the sick, in addition to its military functions, was founded near the Temple in Jerusalem. The Crusades were unmistakably an international movement, but the first Crusade was notable for the participation of French nobles: *gesta Dei per Francos* (the will of God through the Franks).

A warlike king: Louis the Fat

King Philip had taken very little part in the Crusades, having been absorbed in local conflicts and domestic concerns. His son Louis was quite different: despite his portly appearance, he began his reign by restoring security as he put an end to the plunderous raids conducted by the lords of the Ile-de-France and nearby areas. He signed a truce with Henry I Beauclerc, but it was soon broken by the death of Henry's son. Louis VI hastened to put up a candidate of his choice to oppose the natural successor of the king of England. It looked very much as though Germany was about to attack France; whereupon Henry Louis VI convened his *ost,* and went to Saint-Denis to collect his oriflamme—the banner of the French kings—thus effectively deterring Emperor Henry V, who decided, after all, not to proceed further, and went back home.

Heeding the wise advice of his friend Suger, Abbey of Saint-Denis, Louis VI did much to promote the communal movement. The towns, particularly those in the north of France which had become rich through the textile trade, resented having to bear the feudal yoke of lay or ecclesiastical overlords. They revolted and won the right to administer themselves. They were granted a communal charter, defining the duties and rights of the inhabitants of those towns. Louis VI did not accept the re-

Aliénor discovered that, after all, she was in fact too closely related to Louis for her marriage to him to be lawful, and that a matrimonial dispensation had not been requested. She persuaded her husband to ask for an annulment of the marriage. This was duly pronounced, by a council of obliging bishops, in 1152, whereupon Aliénor offered both her hand and her dowry to the Plantagenet Henry II.

By means of a series of successions and marriages, Geoffroi Plantagenet, Count of Anjou, Touraine and Maine, had become Duke of Normandy and pretender to the English throne. He

volt of the bourgeois, severely punishing those in Laon who had massacred the bishop of the town, a real tyrant. Yet he later granted them, and many other small and large towns, charters of freedom; such freedoms were less extensive, but they were certainly a step in the right direction. One of the more famous of these charters is that of Lorris (Gatinais), which was imitated by several other towns. Louis VI and his successors also established new towns, whose inhabitants were not required to pay duties; this is the period when towns with the names *Villefranche* or *Villeneuve*, which are so numerous in France, were founded.

The development of the economy led to an increase in trade and the number of trade fairs; people used to travel a great distance to attend those which were held at Champagne and Saint-Denis.

Anxious to make his sovereign weight felt throughout France and keep the barons under control, the king used to intervene everywhere, even in Auvergne. At the end of his long reign, he had greatly enhanced the royal domains by marrying his son

and successor, Louis, to Aliénor of Aquitaine, whose superb dowry consisted of the splendid province which stretched all the way from Poitou to the Pyrenees.

Capetians versus Plantagenets

Unlike his father, whom he succeeded in 1137, Louis VII was not a very energetic character. He was pious and even scrupulous. In response to an appeal from Saint Bernard, and acting against the advice of his friend Suger, he decided to set off on the second Crusade, as the Holy Land was still threatened by the infidels. Bernard, who had preached in favor of the Crusade at Vézelay, in 1147, was a fervent, hard-hitting Christian, the founder of Clairvaux Abbey, reformer of the Benedictine Order, whose wealth he severely criticized, and an opponent of the philosopher Abélard. Hearing him speak, the feudal lords were carried away by his vehemence. Louis VII decided to take along his wife, Aliénor of Aquitaine, who was not happy with life in her new household, especially after the luxury and the free and easy ways of the court in Aquitaine. During the Crusade,

With the emblem of the Cross emblazoned on their shields, the ironclad knights rush headlong at the Infidel. At a time when the Church and the royal authority forbade private wars among the feudal lords—because of their shattering effect on the rural economy and population— the Crusades enabled the lords to give vent to their warlike instincts, while at the same time earning the remission of their sins.

was never to reign on that throne, but Henry II, his son, was crowned at Westminster in 1154. The Anglo-Angevin empire had been founded; in France, it reached from the Bresle, the river separating Picardie from Normandy, to the Pyrenees, and its sheer size created an intolerable situation for the Capetians, causing a long struggle which, including truces, was to last almost a hundred years.

Louis VII did not always find this situation to his liking, but, while challenging his powerful rival for control of the Vexin, he was able to take a rather clever hand in the conflict be-

tween Henry II and the Archbishop of Canterbury, Thomas à Becket. He also supported the sons of Henry II against their father.

During his reign Gothic art began to flourish. The use of the pointed arch and the flying buttress made it possible to build really tall churches and light them abundantly with the daylight streaming through lavish stained glass windows. Statues became much more beautiful. The magnificent cathedrals of Senlis, Chartres, Reims, Amiens, Rouen, and many others, were built about this time. The first stone of Notre-Dame de Paris

was laid by Bishop Maurice de Sully in 1162. Gothic art should really be called French art: *opus francigenum*. It spread thereafter to the whole of Western Christianity.

Philippe Auguste, collector of land

The reign of Philippe August II got off to a good start, as his marriage to Isabelle de Hainaut made it possible for him to join Artois to the royal domains. He also supported the sons of Henry II Plantagenet against their father, Henry of the Short Cloak, and after the latter's death, Richard Lion-Heart and even Landless John.

This masterpiece of Gothic art, the Cathedral of Reims, which was begun in 1211, was not completed until the beginning of the 14th century. The breadth of its nave and the beauty of its stained glass and its sculptures have made it justly famous. It was contemporary with the reign of Saint Louis, who is seen humbly giving food to the poor (below).
Besides being a saint, he was also a humane, just and peace-loving monarch.

In 1189, Henry II died of grief at Chinon, finding himself abandoned by so many who might have supported him. His successor remained on good terms with the King of France despite the question of Vexin, and, together, both of them decided to set off for the third Crusade. Salah El-Din (Saladin) had just captured Jerusalem, and the Frankish kingdom was in need of help. The king levied a Saladine tithe on those who did not cross themselves; this was in addition to the tithe already levied by the clergy on the faithful. Before leaving France, Philippe created the bailiffs and the seneschals, royal agents, of higher rank than the provosts and the sergeants, who were required not only to admin-

ister the royal domain in their respective bailliages and areas, with judicial, administrative and financial authority, but also to keep a close watch on the fiefs of the great barons, and, when necessary, to intervene in them.

The Crusade was cut short. Philippe returned to France and took advantage of the absence of Richard Lion-Heart, who had been made prisoner on his return from the Holy Land by the Emperor of Germany, in order to ally himself with Richard's younger brother, Landless John, and undertake the conquest of the territory held by the Plantagenets. The release of Richard altered the situation: he defeated the king of France at Freteval

in 1194, after a reconciliation with John. Philip's position was becoming untenable: because he had rejected his second wife, Ingeburge of Denmark, soon after their wedding (for reasons which remain obscure to this day), and then married Agnes de Méran, even though his marriage to Ingeburge had never been annulled, the Pope declared him excommunicated, and laid an interdict on the whole kingdom of France. Richard seemed to be triumphing over the Capetians, and built the citadel of Chateau-Gaillard near Andelys. Fate had ordained, however, that he should be killed in 1199, while laying siege to the seat of a minor Limousin lord, Chalus. His brother and successor, Landless John,

was an invalid, suffering from cyclothymia. He signed the treaty of Le Goulet, near Vernon, with Philippe in 1200. Philippe recovered Vexin, and his son Louis married the niece of Landless John, Blanche of Castille. However, shortly afterwards, in defense of the cause of one of his vassals, he went to war again, and took Chateau-Gaillard, Normandy, Touraine and Anjou. He put his cousin Pierre de Dreux on the throne to replace John's nephew, Arthur, who was been assassinated at Rouen by his uncle.

Meanwhile, in response to the appeal of the Pope, whose legate, Pierre de Castelnau, had been killed by the Albigensian heretics, the lords of northern France embarked on a crusade against Languedoc, in order to eradicate this heresy which had withstood all the preaching of Saint Dominic and the Dominicans. The heretics sought to recover the purity of the early Church and were savagely critical of the clergy with their wealth and facility for compromise. They were supported by the Count of Toulouse. Heeding the appeal of Simon de Montfort, the crusaders streamed south, took Carcassonne and Béziers, and defeated Raimond, Count of Toulouse at the battle of Muret (1213), together with his ally the king of Aragon; yet they were unable to take Toulouse. Philippe Auguste did not participate in the crusade, though he hoped to turn it to his advantage.

In 1214, with the aid of two disloyal lords, Ferrand of Flanders, and Renaud of Burgundy, and, more particularly, with that of the Emperor of Germany, Otto of Brunswick, Landless John sought revenge. He disembarked at La Rochelle, but was defeated at La Roche-aux-Moines, near Angers, while Philippe Auguste won

the splendid victory of Bouvine (1214). Philippe's son, Louis, later tried, in vain, to conquer England; he was forced to abandon the attempt after the death of Landless John.

The closing years of his reign were more tranquil; Philippe became reconciled with Ingeburge, though he did not re-marry her. He enhanced the appearance and security of his capital by building a new outer wall, some traces of which remain.

He died in 1223. This king, who ranks among the greatest of the kings of France, certainly deserves his second name, Auguste. Thanks to him, the royal domain was greatly enlarged (*augere,* in Latin) and the authority of the monarch was strengthened.

A king, a saint

The reign of Louis VIII, the son of Philippe Auguste, husband of Blanche of Castile, was short, but fruitful. The king took a particular interest in the Albigensian affair. Since the death of Simon of Montfort, the heretics had begun to show signs of renewed activity, so Louis VIII decided to mount another crusade against them in 1226. After a long siege, he took Avignon, established seneschals at Beaucaire and Carcassonne. He was on his way back to the capital, in November 1226, when he died, after a brief illness, at Montpensier, in Auvergne.

He left numerous children; Louis, the heir to the throne, was only twelve years of age. His mother, Blanche of Castile, governed the kingdom with a firm hand. She suppressed the revolts of the major barons, such as the Counts of Champagne, Brittany or La Marche, who were helped, to varying degrees, by the king of England, Henry III. She compelled the recently founded university of Paris—Robert

de Sorbon was soon to found the college which bears his name—to bow to her authority. She also married Louis XI to Marguerite of Provence, a move which greatly enhanced the influence of France in the south-east.

One should not think of Saint Louis as a figure on a stained glass window. He was a saint, but also a man. He had been admirably raised by his mother, and astonished his subjects by showing great virtues which were altogether rare at the time. He was evenhanded without being weak, authoritarian but not harsh, generous without excess.

The king's first act was to put an end to the Albigensian affair by signing the Treaty of Meaux-Paris (1229) with the Count of Toulouse, Raimond VI. The Count's daughter married Alphonse, Louis' brother. On the death of the couple, the whole of Languedoc would revert to the royal domain, thus greatly increasing its size. He entrusted Artois to Robert, Poitou to Alphonse and Anjou to Charles, his brothers. These princes, with control over their respective territories, were to be the stem from which new feudal houses would later develop.

Louis IX brought the Duke of Brittany to his senses (1234), and extended his rule in all directions. The Plantagenet Henry III made another attempt to recover his continental domains, but was defeated by Louis at the Taillebourg bridge, near Saintes (1242). In 1259, he signed the Treaty of Paris, with Henry III, putting an end once and for all to the conflict between the Plantagenets and the Capetians: Henry III formally ceded all the provinces conquered by Philippe Auguste, keeping, as his sole territories in France, Aquitaine and certain southwestern areas restored to him by Louis IX. The treaty gave rise to protests in France, as it was felt that Louis could have conquered the whole lot: however, he preferred peace to a latent state of war.

In 1244, he took up the cross. The Latin kingdom in the Orient was rapidly shrinking away. The king of France set sail from Aigues-Mortes to conquer Egypt, so as to be in a position to negotiate the exchange of Egyptian cities and certain cities of Palestine. At first, the Crusade, which began in 1249, was quite successful. Louis IX took Damiette, won the battle of Mansurah, but lost valuable time along the Nile, was forced to make a painful retreat and was eventually taken prisoner. After a large ransom had been paid for his release, he went to Palestine, where he spent three years fortifying the cities of the country, and forging useful alliances with the Ismaelians and the Syrians. After the death of his mother who had been governing the kingdom in his absence (1254), the king returned to France.

Subsequently, he reformed the administration, by setting up a system of royal inspectors who, working in pairs, were to check on the bailiffs and the seneschals, hear complaints from the common people and administer justice promptly. It was about this time that the *Curia Regis,* or royal court, became divided into several organs of government: the Council of the King, the Parliament of Paris, the High Court of Justice (there were other courts in the provinces) and the Chamber of Accounts, which monitored expenditures and prepared the kingdom's budget.

Gothic art was now really at its height. The university of Paris became organized and received its statutes from the Pope.

Louis was a pious man, though without being a bigot. He proved able to stand firm against the demands of the Papal tax-collector, and was generally very independent towards the Holy See, refusing, for example, to intervene in the conflict between Emperor Frederick II and the Papacy. Yet he was constantly haunted by the need to defend the Holy Places. On the advice of his brother Charles of Anjou, who had become Count of Provence, he organized another crusade against Tunis, hoping to cut the Moslem world in two. However, from sheer fatigue, the king died outside the walls of the city on 25 August 1270.

Years before the Church actually canonized him, at the end of the century, Louis was elevated to the status of saint in the minds of the people who bitterly lamented his passing, remembering how he had lowered their taxes and done so much to promote trade. His death marked the high point of the Middle Ages.

A modern king: Philippe the Fair

Philippe III The Bold (1270–1286) lacked the qualities of his father. This weak man, so readily influenced by others, chose as his friend Pierre de La Brosse whom he later had hung for treason. On the death of his brother Alphonse, he reunited the *comté* of Toulouse to the crown, but returned Agenais and Saintonge to the king of England and gave the Pope the Comtat Vanaissin (Avignon). He supported the efforts of his brother, Charles of Anjou, in Sicily. The expedition was not a success, however. The *Sicilian Vespers* (1282) culminated in the massacre of the Angevins. In order to defend his rights in Aragon, which he had obtained through his marriage to the Aragonese heiress, Philippe embarked on a full-scale crusade, but died at Perpignan in 1286.

His son and successor, Philippe IV the Fair, was quite a different sort of person; he surrounded himself with powerful advisers who provided justifications for his frequently arbitrary acts. The *légistes* (Pierre Flote, Nogaret and a number of others) assisted the king in his government.

In the eyes of the king, the interests of the State were supreme. Philippe did not hesitate to seize the English fortresses in the south-west, as he felt they were necessary for the security of his kingdom. He waged war vigorously against the Flemish who, in his opinion, were becoming too independent, having assassinated his representatives (the *Bruges Matins*). Despite an initial defeat, he routed the Flemish forces at Mons-en-Pévèle (1304).

Like his grandfather, Philippe was very adept at accumulating prime real estate for the royal domains. Such additions included Champagne, Navarre and the city of Lyon. His brand of justice was merciless; no sooner had he discovered that his daughters-in-law (Marguerite and Blanche of Burgundy, the wives of his sons) had committed adultery, than he had them locked up. Marguerite died in Chateau-Gaillard, and Blanche withdrew to the abbey of Maubuisson.

Philippe the Handsome organized the Parliament of Paris. He had realized that a kingdom could not live without taxes; whereas the tax known as *aide* had, up till that time, been levied in a very irregular way, he made it into a direct, permanent tax. There were rumblings of discontent: the king thought nothing of lowering the value of the state currency—a notion which, while standard practice today, seemed scandalous to the Frenchmen of the Middle Ages. Certain historians have even used the term "forger" to describe this king; yet, if this is the criterion one is to follow, how many modern governments would stand close scrutiny?

Philippe the Fair decided to tax the clergy as well as the laity. The bishops raised a storm of protest, but to no avail. Pope Boniface VIII, a rather intractable man on such issues, intervened and issued a series of harshly worded Papal Bulls against the recalcitrant monarch. Philippe had his conduct approved, in 1302, by a council of notables (they did not constitute what later came to be known as the *états généraux*); then he sent one of his *légistes*, or senior advisers, Nogaret, to meet the Pope at Anagni. Nogaret struck the Pope, who later died of shame and indignation on account of this incident. His successor, Clement V, was of French origin, and moved the entire Holy See to Avignon, where it stayed for the greater part of the 14th century.

Philippe was constantly in need of money. In order to get it, he attacked the Order of the Knights Templar who, through their system of trading posts which ringed the Mediterranean, had become the bankers of the Western world. The king accused them of every conceivable kind of wrongdoing, and, in 1308, he arrested the Grand Master of the Order, Jacques de Molay, and its main dignitaries. After a long trial, confessions and recantations, they were all condemned to death and burnt alive in Paris. The king seized a part of their property. He died several months later.

The three sons of Philippe the Fair reigned successively, between 1314 and 1328: Louis X, from 1314 to 1316 (his reign was marked by the trial and hanging of Enguerrand de Martigny), Philippe V the Long, from 1316 to 1322, and Charles IV the Fair, from 1322 to 1328.

This was period of conflict with England and conflict with the Flemish—a period in which the French, groaning under a burden of taxation and a prey to unrest, sorely missed the good old days of Saint Louis, when money had really been worth something.

4 The Valois and the Hundred Years' War

None of Philip the Handsome's sons having a male heir, there were now three claimants for the French throne: Philippe of Evreux who, having married Joan of Navarre, was Louis X's son-in-law. He was rejected. Edward III of England whose mother Isabelle was the sister of the deceased kings; he was, therefore, the grandson of Philip the Fair. Lastly, there was Philippe de Valois, who, by his father Charles, was the nephew of the same Philip the Fair and a first cousin of the last three kings. The barons chose the third of these pretenders. At the time, no-one gave thought to the Salic law. Edward III who, though displeased, was extremely busy in England, eventually gave his approval and even rendered homage to the new king of France for his lands in Aquitaine.

Philippe's first military act was the suppression of the revolt of the Flemish, whom he defeated at Mont-Cassel in August 1328. Then, he took a hand in the dispute between Robert d'Artois and his aunt Mahaut. Both the aunt and her daughter disappeared in rather mysterious circumstances. When summoned before the royal court, Robert chose instead to take refuge in England, when he tried to turn Edward against Philippe VI.

In fact, while Philippe merely intended to organize a crusade, Edward constantly sought to harm France. An instance of this is his ban on the export of English wools to France. Finally, in October 1337, he openly challenged Philippe and declared his intention, in writing, to uphold his rights to the crown of France by force of arms.

At this point, in order to thwart the ambitions of the king of England, French jurists invoked the ancient Salic law, whereby women were not allowed to transfer their rights to their husbands.

The French army was made up of the nobility; each noble vassal owed the king forty days of service, after which the king had to pay a certain amount for keeping these men under arms any longer. The nobles fought on horseback; there was also infantry, consisting of mercenaries recruited by captains, and generally despised by the cavalry.

The early stages of the war went badly for France. The French fleet was destroyed at L'Ecluse, in June 1340. Philippe had to go to war against the rebellious Flemish, led by Jacques Artevelde. In Brittany, there was a new war of succession, as the king of France supported Charles de Blois against Jean de Montfort who was aided by the English. Finally, in 1346, Edward landed in Normandy at the head of a powerful army, and, on August 26, routed the French cavalry at the calamitous Battle of Crécy, where the English cross-bowmen proved truly superior. The king of England then turned north and laid siege to Calais, which surrendered in August 1347. The six burghers of Calais who were to have been hung as punishment for the town's resistance were pardoned by the Queen of England. Calais was to remain in English hands

town of Montpellier from the king of Majorca.

Reverses and revolutions

Philippe's son, Jean II, was came to be known as *the Good*. He was extremely devoted to the notion of chivalry, which, through his moral precepts and material dispositions, eventually became an integral part of the Middle Ages. John the Good, a gay chivalrous soul, instituted a new order of chivalry, the Order of the *Etoile* (Star).

However, Edward III had not abandoned his hopes of becoming king of France; moreover, King John was himself in grave difficulties. He soon came into conflict with his son-in-law Charles the Bad, a particularly nasty, vindictive person, whom he eventually had locked up. But Charles later escaped and rose up in arms against his lawful sovereign. The king convened the Estates-General, in order to seek their financial aid. Led by Etienne Marcel, Provost of the merchants of Paris, the Estates agreed to grant subsidies only on condition that they could check on the uses to which they were put; John accordingly had to consent to their terms.

At this moment, the Black Prince, son of Edward III, landed in Aquitaine and headed north; Jean rushed south to meet him. Their two armies collided at Maupertuis, near Poitiers. Once again the French were routed, and by nightfall on 19 September 1356, John was in the custody of the English.

The Dauphin, Charles, was beset with the most extreme difficulties. In response to Etienne Marcel, the Parisians rebelled and massacred the advisers of the Dauphin. Etienne Marcel set up a virtual dictatorship over Paris, while the Black Prince proceeded with

for nearly two centuries.

Philippe convened the *états généraux,* or Estates-General, of the kingdom. This was the first occasion on which the three orders (nobility, clergy and the *tiers état,* or commons) had deliberated together. The situation of France was becoming increasingly desperate: the black plague was rampant among the population and had caused great loss of life. The king came in for some harsh criticism during the meeting of the *états*; how-ever, they did agree to his proposed new tax on salt, the *gabelle,* which was, a short while later, to become highly unpopular, as salt was widely used to preserve perishable foodstuffs.

Philippe VI died in 1350. Under his reign, the province of Dauphiné had been joined to the crown when he had bought the province from the dauphin of Viennois, subject to the condition that, thenceforth, the eldest son of the king of France would take the title of Dauphin. Philippe also bought the

This famous portrait of John the Good (bottom right), done in London about 1359 by Girard d'Orléans, is the earliest authentic representation of a French king. After John's disastrous reign, Charles V, whose coronation is shown here (upper right), set right the defeats and mistakes of the past. He was admirably aided in his endeavors by Bertrand de Guesclin, the valiant Constable, a cast of whose head is shown here, lower left.

the conquest of Poitou and neighboring provinces. And that was not all: outraged at the extortionate demands and the brutality of their overlords, the peasants, under Jacques Karle, attacked and looted the castles of Picardie and Ile-de-France, while Charles the Bad, who had escaped from Rouen, formed an alliance with the English.

The Dauphin succeeded in fleeing from Paris. The peasant revolt was savagely suppressed. Soon, the burghers of Paris began to find Marcel's dictatorship unbearable and killed him. On 8 May 1360, Charles and Edward III signed the Treaty of Brétigny, separating France from Poitou, Aunis, Saintonge, Quercy, Rouergue and Agenais. However, peace had been restored and John the Good was released.

Feeling ill at ease in France, he returned to London, on the pretext that his son Louis, who had been held as

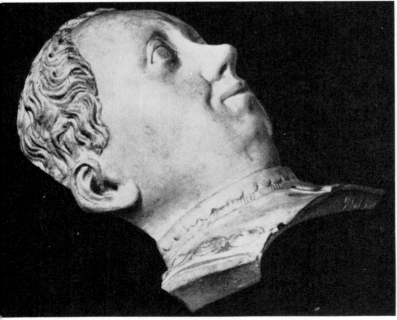

The Château de Vincennes, at the gates of Paris, was always one of the favorite residences of the French kings, as far back as the time of Saint Louis, who liked to rest and administer justice there. However, it was Charles V who had a particular preference for Vincennes; he undertook the reconstruction of the entire château, the chapel and the enormous dungeon, which he did not live to see completed. The Château de Vincennes is closely linked with the history of France.

hostage by the English, had escaped. He died there in 1364.

Charles V, a wise and clever king
That left Charles the Bad. In May 1364, he was defeated at Cocherel by du Guesclin, shortly before the crowning of the new king of France, and was thereafter obliged to give up the struggle. The reign of Charles V began in the most auspicious manner, but France lay in ruins and devastation. Companies of mercenaries roamed the countryside at will, looting as they went. The Treaty of Gué-rande had put an end to the war in Brittany. Charles had recognized the Duke of Brittany, John IV, in return for the latter's offer of homage to him as sovereign. Du Guesclin undertook to remove the groups of brigands, by taking them closer to the Spanish border, in order to defend Henri de Trastamare. In the process, he was taken prisoner, to be released only when Charles V paid his ransom.

Through a number of skilful financial measures, in particular the regular collection of the *fouage*, or tax on fires or families, the king restored the financial and economic situation of the kingdom. Agriculture once more prospered. He also re-organized the army, and gradually resumed hostilities against the English, using, for the first time, a type of guerrilla tactics which was to prove highly effective. The towns which were occupied by English garrisons rebelled and drove them out; despite all their efforts, the English were obliged to withdraw. At the end of his reign, their sole remaining possessions in France were Aquitaine, Cherbourg, Brest, La Rochelle and Calais. The initiatives taken by the Black Prince had ended in disaster.

Du Guesclin had been promoted to

the rank of High Constable of France. Yet he was to refuse to help the king annex Brittany, and the whole endeavor came to nought.

This frail, sickly-looking monarch, who was happier among his books than on the battle-field, was also a patron of the arts. During his reign, many *châteaux* and palaces were built: Vincennes (his birthplace) which he completed, the Louvre, the Bastille, Beauté-sur-Marne, to name but a few.

By the end of his reign, the currency had become stable, and prosperity had returned. One wonders, though,

whether he had been right to give whole territories to his brothers; he had given Burgundy to Philippe, who had distinguished himself at the battle of Poitiers, Anjou to Louis and Bourbonnais and Berry to John.

Charles V died at Vincennes, on 13 September 1380. His son, Charles VI, was only twelve years of age.

The mad king

France was then governed by the king's uncles, who were primarily concerned with their own interests. Philippe the Bold, Duke of Burgundy and Count of Flanders by his marriage, struck at the Flemish, who had rebelled yet again (the victory of Roosebeke). After his marriage to Isabelle of Bavaria, Charles VI resumed control and governed with the

help of the Marmousets, a team of keen young administrators, who were determined to bring about certain reforms. However, on his way through the forest of Le Mans to subdue a rebellious vassal, the king had a fit and momentarily lost his mental powers. As these fits became more and more frequent, the uncles took power once again.

They were soon at loggerheads among themselves, and were particularly hostile to Charles' brother, Louis d'Orleans. After the accession to power of Fearless John, Duke of Burgundy, who was jealous of his cousin Louis d'Orleans, this rivalry became particularly intense. The struggle reached such a violent pitch that John had Louis assassinated in 1407. France then was divided into

The funeral of Charles VI. *This 15th-century miniature is taken from the* Vigiles de Charles VII *(a prayerbook). A gentle expression on his face, and his body clad in the trappings of royalty, the poor mad king is taken to Saint-Denis on a catafalque carried aloft. A reign which had been disastrous for France had come to an end.*

This picture of king Charles VII is certainly a good likeness. The monarch has that melancholy, gloomy look which was justified by so much of what had happened. For more than ten years he had been an exile from his capital and had merely been king of Bourges. Gradually, Charles shook himself out of his torpor and, with the help of Yolande of Aragon and Agnes de Sorel, the king was to become Charles VII, the Victorious.

Joan of Arc's house in Domremy, a small village on the border of Lorraine and Champagne. Joan of Arc's house was restored and modified during the second half of the 15th century.

two camps, on the one hand, the Bourguignons, who tried to justify the murder, and on the other, the Armagnacs, under High Constable Bernard d'Armagnac, son-in-law of Charles, the new Duke of Orleans.

The Bourguignons won control of Paris. Yet Fearless John had to bow to the demands of the community of butchers, who were incensed at the high-handed ways of these selfish and brutal princes. Fearless John tried to take advantage of this revolutionary movement (1413) which was led by Caboche, a butcher, and accepted the decree known as the *ordonnance cabochienne,* which met the terms laid down by the butchers and the merchants. Shortly afterwards, however, Bernard d'Armagnac took Paris, when the Duke of Burgundy had fled it, and imposed on the capital a full-scale dictatorship.

This was the moment which the king of England chose to resume his plans for conquest. As he had done on

previous occasions, he landed in Normandy. The Battle of Agincourt (October 25, 1415) which was a disaster for the French cavalry, showed that they had learnt nothing from the defeats of Crécy and Poitiers-Maupertuis.

The years which followed are among the darkest of the whole of the history of France. While Henry V proceeded with his methodical conquest of Normandy, the two eldest heirs of the mad king died. The Dauphin now became Charles, Count of Ponthieu, who was protected by the energetic and ardent Duchess of Anjou, Yolande of Aragon. In 1417, the Duke of Burgundy took Paris by a trick. The Armagnacs were massacred. On the advice of Yolande, Charles attempted a reconciliation with Fearless John. Their meeting, which took place on the bridge at Montereau, quickly got out of hand: Jean was assassinated (1419). His son and successor, Philippe the Good,

alined himself with the English who were already masters of Champagne and of part of Ile-de-France. The Duke of Burgundy persuaded Isabelle of Bavaria and the poor mad king to sign the Treaty of Troyes (1420), which violently condemned Charles, called him an upstart, alleging that he was, in any case, illegitimate, and therefore not the real Dauphin, and yielded Normandy to the king of England, who married one of the daughters of Charles VI. The child who was to emerge from that union, the future Henry VI, was to be king of both France and England.

Yet France was far from entirely conquered. The Loire valley had held out; in fact, Yolande inflicted a severe defeat on the English at Vieil-Baugé in 1421. Henry V died at Vincennes in 1422, leaving a son who was only a few months old. The Duke of Bedford was made Regent. Charles VI was to follow the king of England to the grave some months later.

Charles VII the Victorious

The Dauphin Charles, who had now become Charles VII, lived in the valley of the Loire, at Chinon or Bourges, where, in 1425, he married Marie d'Anjou, daughter of Yolande. This "king of Bourges", as he was called, was recognized by much of France: Poitou, Auvergne, Languedoc, Provence (which belonged to the Duke of Anjou). He was still able to count on the services of troops and worthy captains, such as La Hire, Xaintrailles or Dunois, though these latter were never particularly successful when confronted with the English. In 1428, the Duke of Bedford decided to dispose, once and for all, of this self-styled king, whose reputation was gravely tarnished by rumors about the circumstances of his birth. He laid siege to Orleans.

A simple peasant girl, Joan of Arc, from Lorraine, a territory in which certain enclaves still belonged to the king of France, suddenly burst upon the scene. She had heard voices from Heaven, ordering her to drive the English out of France and have the king crowned at Reims. The supernatural character of her mission was undisputed. With a small escort, she set out for Chinon, disclosed to the king that he was truly a son of France, entered Orleans and liberated the town in a matter of a few days, on 8 May 1429. She won the battle of Patay, and took the king to Reims where he was solemnly crowned in September. She was to continue her heroic struggle until her capture outside Compiegne. After a shameful ecclesiastical trial conducted by Archbishop Cauchon, of Beauvais, a man who was wholly committed to the English cause, Joan was delivered to her enemies and burned at the stake, as a witch, heretic and an apostate, at Rouen, on May 29, 1431. She was re-habilitated in 1450 and canonized in 1920.

Charles had some difficulty shaking off his apathy. However, he did achieve a reconciliation with the Duke of Burgundy; the English were driven out of Paris and the king was able to make a triumphal entry into the city.

He benefited greatly, in his endeavors, from the assistance of a merchant from Bourges, a man of immense drive and initiative: Jacques Cœur. This was a man who had set up his own trading posts throughout the Mediterranean and in the main cities of France. He was a financial wizard who did much to restore order to the royal coffers. Eventually, his enormous wealth was the cause of downfall: after a rather dubious trial, he was sentenced to imprisonment, but managed to escape. He was one of the most original figures of the 15th century.

Charles and the Pope concluded the Pragmatic Sanction, of Bourges, which defined the freedoms and duties of the Church of France (1438).

The feudal lords, who were unhappy about the measures taken involving them, rebelled against the authority of the king. This was the *Praguerie* (so named by analogy with the Prague uprising). However, this league was soon reduced to impotence.

Yolande of Aragon was now dead. Charles was a new man, with new spirit, thanks to his mistress, the pretty Agnes Sorel. In 1445, he signed a truce with his adversary Henry VI of England; this provided him with an opportunity to re-design his army, in such a way as to have available, at all times, well-equipped, battle-ready troops, while simultaneously putting an end to the right of the nobles to raise armies on their own.

This meant that, in 1450, the king was prepared to resume the struggle against England. Many towns in Ile-de-France and Normandy had already risen in opposition to the English. With some outstanding military leaders, such as Richemont, under his command, Charles defeated the English at the battle of Formigny (Cotentin). Very soon, the whole of Normandy was liberated. Two years later, another victory, at Castillon, near Bordeaux, enabled Charles the Victorious to take Aquitaine, a prize which had long eluded the French. The only English possession in the entire country was now Calais.

But war was not Charles' only concern; with the assistance of his advisers, such as Pierre de Brézé, he set about re-organizing administration

This 15th-century miniature gives one an idea of the opulence of the court of Charles the Bold, the powerful Duke of Burgundy, rival to Louis XI. The king, however, won in the end.

and justice. A decree issued in 1454 set forth the competence and composition of the Parliament of Paris, the highest court of justice.

The closing years of his reign were marred somewhat by the attitude of the Dauphin, Louis, who, on several occasions, conspired against his father, and eventually fled to Flanders, to seek refuge with the Duke of Burgundy. Undeterred, Charles pressed ahead with his plans for France's recovery. After so many years of foreign and civil wars, the kingdom was truly a shambles.

"The universal spider"

Louis XI was active, authoritarian, energetic, clever and at times devious; his piety, moreover, was often motivated by self-interest. One chronicler used the term *l'universelle aragne* to describe him, because, like the spider, he wove his web in all directions.

His first act was to rid himself of all the former followers of his father, even old Dunois, who had once been the companion of Joan of Arc, preferring, instead, men from the lesser nobility, such as Jean Bourré, his major financier, or even commoners, like his close associate Olivier le Daim, a barber whom he made one of his advisers.

The king's financial measures caused rumblings of discontent among the majority of the nobles, who formed a common front against him, in what came to be known as the War of the Public Good—a rather curious title. Louis XI met the rebels in battle at Monthéry, on 16 July 1465. The outcome was indecisive; eventually, the king granted certain concessions, in the treaties of Saint-Maur and Conflans, to the more powerful among the nobles involved.

This grandson of Yolande of Aragon wished to extend his kingdom beyond the Pyrenees, and did, in fact, succeed in occupying Roussillon for several years. But his major concern was to recover the towns in the Somme region—Arras, Péronne—as a protection for his northern frontier. At the time, these towns were in the hands of Charles the Bold, the powerful Duke of Burgundy, whose ambition was to create a huge state of his own, and become the great duke of the Western world. Two men met at Péronne. Meanwhile, however, Louis XI had secretly incited a town in Flanders to revolt against Charles, who, being informed about it during the meeting, locked the king up, and forced him to sign a humiliating treaty which Louis XI was never to fulfil.

Charles tried to conquer new provinces. In 1472, he advanced as far as Beauvais, but the defenders of the town, under the inspired leadership of Jeanne Hachette, drove him back.

Thereafter, Louis XI concentrated on getting others to do his fighting for him.

His brand of justice was harsh: Cardinal Balue and the Bishop of Verdun, who had conspired against the king, were locked up in narrow iron cells, jokingly known as Louis XI's "little girls".

In 1475, the new king of England, Edward IV, attempted one last move in France. It failed, whereupon Louis XI and he signed the treaty of Picquigny: in return for definitively ceding his continental territories, Edward received the amounts of money which he needed.

The kingdom was soon to swell considerably. Charles the Bold, who had been beaten by the Swiss at Granson and Morat (1476), and also by the Duke of Lorraine, René II, died outside the walls of Nancy in January 1477. Louis XI then seized Burgundy. He cast covetous glances towards Flanders, but had to content himself with the treaty of Arras (1482), whereby the twelve-year-old Dauphin was betrothed to Marguerite, daughter of Marie de Bourgogne and Maximilian of Austria, the grand-daughter of Charles the Bold.

Meanwhile, Louis added to the royal possessions Anjou and Provence, which had been bequeathed to him by the good king René (1480). Louis XI died in 1483. Throughout his life, he had worked tirelessly for the good of his country; he had restored monuments, revived agriculture, encouraged the first industrial enterprises, the mines, he had repaired the roads and established the postal service. Notwithstanding his faults, he was a very great monarch.

44

This portrait of the famous knight Bayard is clearly the work of a later period. With his exemplary fidelity and courage, it was Bayard who knighted King Francis I on the evening of the battle of Marignan.

This portrait painted on wood shows King Charles VIII. Like his predecessors, the monarch is wearing his hair long; yet styles have changed—the shirt is now much more open and the fur-lined coat is extremely elegant.

The end of the Middle Ages

The Dauphin Charles, who had now become Charles VIII, was only thirteen years old. His elder sister Anne, wife of Pierre de Beaujeu, was made Regent; she was a lively and clever woman, who, in the words of Louis XI, had the "heart of a man in the body of a woman".

The 300-or-so deputies meeting in the Estates-General at Tours granted her wide powers. However, some feudal lords were still prepared to challenge the royal authority, first and foremost the Duke of Brittany.

For almost the whole of the Middle Ages, Brittany was been virtually independent. Its dukes offered merely a simple form of homage. During the Hundred Years' War, they wavered between France and England, or remained prudently neutral. Duke Francis II, however, having no male heir, was extremely worried about the fate of his duchy.

In 1485, together with a number of other malcontents, he revolted against the power of the Regent; in the ensuing conflict, which was known as the *Mad War,* Anne was effortlessly victorious. Nevertheless, she did make some concessions, to both nobility and people, by reducing certain taxes and also by deciding to draft and print a repertory of the customs of each province which lay at the basis of the law.

In 1488, François II went to war yet again, and sought the aid of the English. He was defeated at Saint-Aubin-du-Cormier. After the Duke's death, his daughter Anne tried hard to find a prince to defend her – but to no avail. Charles VIII laid siege to Rennes. Anne agreed to marry him, on condition that Brittany would be united to France solely through his person. All the great feudal estates had disappeared, and the kingdom was now prosperous and strong.

From his great-uncle, King René of Anjou, Charles VIII had inherited undisputed rights to the kingdom of Naples. Having secured the neutrality of his neighbors (at a high price), Charles then set about the conquest of Naples, which turned out to be a fairly easy matter. However, almost all the Italian princes united against the king of France. The king brought back with him works of art, furniture, and, above all, artists who were to introduce into France the first artistic accomplishments of the Renaissance.

Charles VIII died at Blois in 1498. He left no male heir for Anne.

CHARLES

5 Wars with Italy, Wars of Religion, the Renaissance

France at the beginning of the 15th century

Certain barely perceptible changes heralded the approach of a new era: great discoveries, such as the printing press, the compass, gunpowder, were to make books more widely available, to facilitate the quest for new lands overseas, and to change the art of warfare.

The organization of society remained basically the same. The king was still the supreme sovereign, legislating by means of decrees and edicts. He was surrounded by a council. The Parliament of Paris and the provincial Parliaments were the highest juridical organs. The Chambre des Comptes audited the income and expenditure of the State. However, when the king so wished, he could convene the Estates-General of the kingdom, who had been known, at times, to be rather difficult. In the provinces, the king was represented by a governor, whose authority was often great. In provinces such as the Dauphiné, Languedoc, Brittany, the provincial states voted and distributed the budget taxes.

The feudal lords tried, when circumstances permitted, to get back their lost power. While serfdom was definitely on the way out, the peasants were still bound by the admission of loyalty and the compulsory form of census which they were required to submit. Despite the great demands which were still made on them, their material situation was improving.

The towns were expanding. Many of them were administered by a municipal magistrate, consul or town council. The merchants formed powerful trade associations. The middle class began to assume a particular importance. Industrial enterprises, mines and quarries all begin to make their appearance, though they were still on a modest, craft level.

Several towns had universities which were attended by thousands of students. The universities of Orleans, Toulouse, Montpellier and, above all, Paris, had the highest reputations.

Louis XII, father of his people

Charles VIII had no direct heir. The crown passed smoothly to his cousin Louis d'Orleans, great-grand-son of Charles V. Louis XI had forced him to marry his daughter Jeanne, who, though a good soul, was lame and hunch-backed. Louis succeeded in having the marriage annulled (1498), and was thus free to marry the widow of Charles VIII. In this way, Brittany remained bound to France. Anne gave him a daughter, Claude.

The king's financial policy was sound. He further lowered the land tax, thus promoting agriculture. However, his Italian policy proved costly, and caused him at times to mortgage off various plots of land from the royal domain. He created new administrative and judicial posts which he sold to the highest bidder, and also arranged to borrow money.

Louis XII revived Charles VIII's Italian ambitions. Besides the kingdom of Naples, he also had designs on the Duchy of Milan, on the pretext that his grandmother Valentine Visconti held certain rights over this territory. In 1499 he took Genoa, in 1500 the duchy of Milan, and, with the aid of the king of Aragon, seized the kingdom of Naples, from which he was expelled in 1501.

Foolishly, he had his daughter Claude betrothed to the heir to Burgundy. He realized the danger of a merger between Brittany and Burgundy, and the Estates-General at Tours dispensed him from his commitments. Claude married her cousin, the future Francis I.

Pope Julian II formed a Holy Alliance of Italian princes against the French; soon, Milan and Genoa were lost.

Despite these costly expeditions, Louis XII really did try to improve the lot of his people. He was a patron of the arts who also contributed to the growth of the artistic Renaissance. His popular title, "father of his people", was well merited.

A knight-king: Francis I

Once again, the throne was vacant, as Louis XII had left no male heir. The crown therefore passed to his son-in-law and cousin, François d'Angoulême, who was also a great-grandson of Charles V. He was to reign from 1515 to 1547 as Francis I.

His reign got off to a spectacular start. In a resolute attempt to recover the duchy of Milan, he crossed the Alps and defeated the Swiss, who were fighting for the Holy Alliance, at Marmont (1515). On the evening following this magnificent victory, Francis was made a knight by the most noble of them all: Bayard. He and the Swiss signed a perpetual peace, the Pope abandoned the struggle and concluded the Concordat of Bologna, granting the king of France a large measure of control over his clergy. Charles, the new king of Spain, decided to accept the kingdom of Naples, in exchange for the Duchy of Milan.

Charles V, great-grandson of Charles the Bold, was not only king of Spain, Duke of Austria, master of Flanders and of almost the whole of Italy, he was also elected Emperor in 1519. His States encircled France. In order to lessen the pressure, Francis I tried to find an ally in the king of Eng-

This portrait of Francis I, by Clouet, is hardly flattering. Francis I was a tough, vigorous man who fought tenaciously against Charles the Fifth and eventually triumphed over him.

François Rabelais, who was born near Chinon, was a brilliant medical student. The author of Gargantua and Pantagruel remains one of the most brilliant and original minds of the French Renaissance.

land, whom he invited to meet him at the camp at Drap d'or, in a splendid display of hospitality. But Henry VIII decided to give his preference to the Emperor. In addition, Francis I alienated the High Constable of Bourbon, one of the most powerful nobles in the kingdom by bringing an action for treason against him, on the grounds that he had engaged in dealings with Charles V. He fled. His property was confiscated, but the king thereafter had one more enemy to cope with.

To defend the duchy of Milan, Francis I set off once more for Italy, where he was soundly defeated at the battle of Pavia (1525). The king himself was taken prisoner. He had to sign the treaty of Madrid, ceding Burgundy to his enemy; this treaty, however, was never carried out, and the peace of Cambrai gave Burgundy to Francis, who abandoned his Italian ambitions. Now a widower, after the death of Claude de France, the king married the sister of Charles V in 1531.

To enhance his security, Francis I formed an alliance with the German princes and began negotiations with the Turks which were only to reach fruition under Charles IX. He built the port of Le Havre, encouraged Jacques Cartier, who discovered Canada, and New-France of America. The silk industry prospered in Lyon at the expense of Italian production. Administration was improving.

The war against Charles V, the ally of Henry VIII, resumed in 1536, and lasted until 1543. After driving the Emperor out of Provence, which he had invaded, Francis I took Nice. He won again at Cerisoles, in Italy. Finally, the treaties of Crédy and Arras put an end to these long wars. France abandoned its claims to Savoy and recovered Burgundy, which the English had seized.

This prolonged warfare had cost a lot of money; the king had had to arrange for loans from the bankers. It was also during his reign that the struggle began against the reformers who were supported by his sister "Marguerite of the daisies". Francis I was also a patron of the arts who protected writers, founded the Collège de France and built many *châteaux* in the new style: Chambord, Blois (the wing named after Francis I), Fontainebleau and Rambouillet, where he died in 1547.

The Renaissance

This name is used to denote a number of innovations which changed both taste and way of life during the reign of Francis I.

In the arts, it took the form of the end of the Gothic style, and the adoption of new decorative motifs, often imitated from Antiquity. Architecture was changing too: layout became simpler, with big bay windows which let in plenty of air and sun. Beauty of appearance was a prime concern everywhere. Francis I arranged for Leonardo da Vinci to come to France; the great artist was to die near Amboise.

In the world of letters, the Schoolmen ceased to dominate learning, and there was a resurgence of interest in Greek and Roman Antiquity. The poetic art was renewed by Marot, and above all Ronsard; their work was followed by a whole host of other poets. Rabelais, under his jocular style, was often a moralist. However, this Renaissance affected only the upper reaches of society, and, to a lesser extent, the bourgeoisie, while its effect on the mass of the people was virtually nil. On the other hand, the Reformation was to disturb the whole of French society profoundly.

The Reformation

The Catholic Church was passing through a grave crisis; as early as the end of the 14th century, the Great Western Schism (1378–1417), with open conflict between rival Popes, had given rise to widespread anxiety. The Popes of the Renaissance were certainly not models of piety. In France, the wealth of the clergy aroused the envy of a nobility which had been im-

There are several pictures of the disastrous battle of Pavia (25 February 1525), at the end of which King Francis I was taken prisoner by the troops of Charles the Fifth: "Everything is lost, save honor!", he wrote to his mother, Louise of Savoy, whose energy saved the kingdom of France. After Pavia, all the king's fanciful hopes evaporated. The struggle against Charles the Fifth was to go on for a long time.

poverished by wars and of a bourgeoisie which valued material gain. The Concordat of Bologna, by permitting the king to appoint bishops and the abbots of monasteries, had done nothing to improve matters. Too many bishops and too many abbots (or Mother Superiors) neglected their flocks or the members of their orders. The *curés*, with their inadequate education, often moved away from their parishes altogether. The Christian faith had declined, partly because of increasingly slack moral attitudes.

Reform was badly needed. In Germany, Luther had broken away from the Catholic Church. In France, a young cleric, Jean Calvin, imitated

him. He preached a return to the purity of the early Church, the abandonment of certain forms of worship, poverty of the clergy, but also, and above all, he challenged various basic dogmas, such as the True Presence of Jesus Christ in the Eucharist.

His preaching met with a favorable response and quickly won new disciples. His doctrines were advocated even in the Court, where pamphlets offensive to the Church were discovered. Then the Church counter-attacked. Calvin had to leave France and take refuge in Geneva. But the reformed religion had been born; it spread throughout the country, in the south, west and elsewhere. At first,

some of the reformers did not seem to have broken away completely from the Church, which was itself in the process of seeking ways to reform, by means of the Council of Trent. Though originally a religious dispute, this was soon going to spill over into the political sphere, and divide the kingdom.

Henry II

Henry II was the husband of Catherine de Medicis, the daughter of a prominent Florentine banker; they had ten children. This rather weak monarch was very much under the influence of his mistress, Diane de Poitiers, and also of the High Constable

François Clouet is also the author of this portrait of Diane de Poitiers, the mistress whom Henry II loved with such passion. Right: portrait of Queen Catherine de Medicis next to her husband, King Henry II.

of Montmorency, and, particularly, of François de Guise. The Guise were remote descendants of the French King John II the Good (through king René of Anjou and his grandson René II, Duke of Lorraine). François de Guise was an ardent Catholic, and he encouraged Henry II, who intended to defend the Church against the Reformation, to set up special tribunals to judge the reforms; the first burnings date from about this time.

There was a renewed outbreak of war against England and Spain. Henry occupied the towns of Metz, Toul and Verdun, which protected his northeastern frontier, with the agreement of the German princes. In order to make up for the inadequate levels of taxation, he issued a bond, "le Grand Parti", which was won favor with the public.

Encouraged by these developments, Henry II took François de Guise to Italy, in an attempt to retake Naples. The Emperor abdicated, and his, successor, Philip II, won the battle of Saint-Quentin (1556). Having been appointed Lieutenant-General

of the kingdom, François de Guise drove back the Spaniards, and captured Calais from the English. By now, however, the coffers of the State were empty: the "Grand Parti" bond could not be repaid. Bankruptcy ensued. Henry II then signed the treaty of Cateau-Cambresis (1559), which gave France Metz, Toul, Verdun and Calais.

During all these wars, the Reformation had been moving steadily ahead, and could now claim many supporters among the nobility, and even princes, such as the king of Navarre, Antoine de Bourbon. The first Protestant synod was held in Paris in 1559.

Wars were not the only feature of Henry II's reign. The terms of reference of the King's Council were more precisely defined, four secretariats of State were set up; moreover, in order to bridge the gap between judges and judged, the king instituted the *présidiaux*, an intermediate court, between the lower courts and the Parliaments.

During a tournament in June 1559,

Henry II was struck by an ill-judged-blow from the lance of Montgomery. He died ten days later.

Thirty years of war

His son, Francis II, was only fifteen years old. The young husband of Mary Stuart was very much under the influence of his mother, Catherine de Medicis and the Guise family. In order to remove him from his influence, a Protestant captain, La Renaudie, hatched a plot, with certain other conspirators, near Amboise. However, their plan was discovered and the ringleader and his associates killed ruthlessly. The person really responsible for the conspiracy was Antoine de Bourbon, king of Navarre, the prince of Condé, Admiral de Coligny and his brothers. Condé was sentenced to death (1560), but was saved by the unexpected death of Francis II, on 5 December.

He was succeeded by his young brother Charles, who was only ten years old. Catherine de Medicis became regent. She was to remain, for many years, the "governess" of

49

France, struggling vainly to keep some sort of balance between the Protestants, who were showing increasing audacity, and the Catholics, who were becoming increasingly fanatical. A civil war, lasting thirty years, was to break out in the kingdom.

Drawing on the aid of the wise chancellor Michel de l'Hospital, who was anxious to reconcile Frenchmen, Catherine de Medicis proved to be very clever in her sincere attempts to keep the peace, and not unduly scrupulous about the means she used to this end. Even so, she failed. The meeting at Poissy (1561) between Catholic and Protestant theologians was a failure. The edict of tolerance promulgated by Catherine displeased the Catholics, and a triumvirate,

formed of Francis de Guise, the High Constable of Montmorency and the Marshal of Saint-André, made them decide to act on their own. The massacre, by François de Guise, of peasants who had gathered to worship at Wassy sparked off a series of civil wars.

These wars were notable for the atrocities which were committed. While the leaders were French, the soldiers were often foreign mercenaries, German *reiters* who plundered, raped and slaughtered wherever they went. The people were the hapless victims of these wars. The reformers took their vengeance by sacking churches and cathedrals. Both sides appealed for help from abroad: the Catholics to the Spaniards, and the reformers to the Protestant German princes. The struggle continued throughout 1562–1563. The Edict of Pacification of Amboise suspended the war, and allowed the Protestants freedom of worship in certain towns and under certain conditions. But matters did not end there: the fighting started again. In 1567, the Protestants tried to take Meaux. The peace of Longjumeau restored the terms of the Edict of Amboise. Again, it was no more than a truce: the war broke out once more. Led by Henry de Guise (known as the *Balafré*, Scarface) and Henry d'An-

In order to protect the young king, Francis II, from the influence of the de Guise, a reformer, La Renaudie, organized a conspiracy in 1560, but it failed. La Renaudie was killed and his companions were hung (top left). Right: a picture of King Henry III, under whose reign France was torn by a great many civil wars. Bottom left: the seal of Marie de Medicis.

This painting by François Dubois dates from the time of the St. Bartholomew's Day massacre. With a gripping, realistic style, it shows the killing of the reformers, ordered by Catherine de Medicis and her son Charles IX.

jou, the young brother of Charles IX, the Catholic army triumphed over the Protestants at Jarnac and Moncontour (1569). Condé died in this engagement, but the skill of Admiral de Coligny saved the reformers and the Edict of Saint-Germain (1570) restored the peace, by granting the reformers four safe havens, including La Rochelle, and a greater degree of freedom.

It was decided that Henri de Na- varre, a Protestant prince, son of Jeanne and Antoine de Bourbon, should marry Marguerite, sister of Charles IX. The Protestants were assuming ever greater power, to the great distress of the Guise family; Admiral de Coligny exerted great influence over Charles IX, who would have preferred to have governed alone. Catherine de Medicis was worried. An attempt on Coligny's life failed. Catherine then persuaded her son to massacre all the Protestants who were to assemble in Paris for the wedding of Marguerite and Henri de Navarre: the ensuing slaughter of several thousand Protestants, on 24 August 1572, came to acquire gruesome celebrity in History as the St. Bartholomew's Day's Massacre. The killing went on for several days afterwards in the provinces. Catherine's policy of alliance with Catholic Spain could now be resumed.

Catherine de Medicis is here shown at prayer in her chapel. The queen, who was the mother of three kings, tried hard to bring religious peace to France. Failing in her endeavors, she massacred the reformers: on Saint Bartholomew's Day.

France was the scene of uncontrollable civil wars. Driven out of his capital, Henry III had to take refuge in Touraine. The League, consisting of the most fanatical Catholics, was the master of Paris. In order to enflame the zeal of the people, the members of the League held a great number of religious ceremonies, with a vast amount of preaching. In this scene, we see a procession moving through the streets of the capital.

Willy-nilly, Henri de Navarre had to become converted, as the Protestant cause seemed lost. But Charles IX, who had given the order for the massacre, died two years later, stricken with remorse. One should not forget that his reign was marked by the signing of a treaty of alliance with the Turks, the Capitulations, credit for which has long been attributed to Francis I.

Charles' brother, Henri III, who had been chosen as king by the Poles, hastened to return to France. This nervous man, with his effeminate ways, surrounded himself with minions who lived with him. Even so, Henri III was both intelligent and courageous. Yet he could not decide on a policy for handling a France which was, more than ever before, torn apart by rival factions. The religious wars were inhuman. The atrocities of men like Monluc, the Catholic leader, or the Baron des Adrets,

leader of the Protestants, have become only too famous.

Henri III first attempted a reconciliation with his young brother François d'Alençon, Duke of Anjou, who was jealous of him; they signed the Peace of Monsieur (1576). The financial situation of the kingdom, which was deplorable, induced the king to issue the Edict of Beaulieu, giving the reformers freedom of worship, except in Paris, and restoring their safe havens which the Saint Bartholomew's Day Massacres had taken away from them (La Rochelle, Montauban, etc.). In another concession, he agreed to the establishment of joint Chambers in which Catholic and Protestant judges would sit.

The war was over, but peace had not returned. Catherine de Medicis made a vain attempt at a reconciliation with her son-in-law Henri de Navarre, who had escaped from the Louvre and become leader of the reformers in the southwest. In need of money, Henri III convened the Estates-General at Blois in December 1576. They granted him the subsidies he requested, though not without condemning his policies first.

To placate the Catholics, a new Edict, that of Poitiers, imposed further restrictions on the freedoms which had been granted to the reformers. The struggle then resumed, all the more bitterly in that the death of the Duke of Anjou (1585) meant that Henri de Navarre was now the heir to the throne, as Henri III had had no children. The French would never accept a Protestant king. A League headed by Henri le Balafré, Duc de Guise, grouped together all the fanatical Catholics who were vehemently opposed to the future successor of Henri III. As this League called on the Spaniards for assistance, and the king

of Navarre appealed to the German princes, the civil war quickly became a foreign war.

In order to satisfy the Duc de Guise, Henri III sent an army against the King of Navarre. The future Henri IV defeated this army at Coutras, but failed to take advantage of his success, as he was loth to use the German *reiters* who had been sent to him. In the west, the war looked like dragging on for ever.

The Duc de Guise was clearly exceeding his authority and made no secret of his contempt for Henri III. In order to dispose of him once and for all, Henri the king forbade him to come to Paris, which was entirely open to the members of the League. Scarface promptly set out for the capital, where he was acclaimed by the inhabitants, who erected barricades against the troops who were faithful to Henri III. The Day of the Barricades (12 May 1588) brought matters to a

head. The king succeeded in fleeing from Paris, and taking refuge in Blois, where he convened the Estates-General in December. Now in control of the capital, Henri de Guise had the gall to attend the meeting of the Estates-General; the king had him and his brother the cardinal murdered on December 24, 1588.

Paris rebelled and closed its doors to the king, appointing a new leader in the person of the Duc de Mayenne, Scarface's brother. Henri III became reconciled with his brother-in-law Henri de Navarre; together, at the head of Catholic and Protestant troops, they set out for Paris, and laid siege to the city.

On August 1, 1589, Henri III was assassinated by a mad monk, Jacques Clément, at his quarters at St-Cloud. What fate lay in store for the hapless kingdom of France, now more severely divided than ever before?

6 Henry IV and Louis XIII

The conquest of the kingdom

Henri, King of Navarre, who had been born at Pau in 1553, had been brought up in the reformed religion. Though he had been forced into Catholicism after the Saint Bartholomew Day Massacre, he had quickly rejoined Calvinism as soon as he could get out of Paris. Devoted to the ideals of peace and tolerance, he had had to fight against the League. He was separated from his wife, Marguerite de Valois, who soon found that separation was not such a bad thing. He lived the good life in Béarn and Navarre, regions loyal to him. This amiable, easy-going man became King of France under the title Henri IV (the Bourbons were descended from Robert, son of Saint Louis). The only trouble was that he was a king with neither a crown nor a kingdom.

The Catholic leaders who had surrounded Henri III denied their support to the new king, who had to lift the siege of Paris. He then headed for Normandy, and defeated the Duc de Mayenne, chief of the League, in a series of battles at Arques, near Dieppe. Then, in March 1589, Henri won handsomely at Ivry, with the cry: "Rally round my white plume!" He tried, in vain, to capture Paris. He took Chartres and Noyon, but had to withdraw from the engagement outside Rouen. Much of France was still hostile to him; moreover, his affair with Gabrielle d'Estrées wasted too much of his time, as his close adviser, Maximilian de Béthune, the future Duc de Sully, repeatedly pointed out to him.

Henri IV realized that this situation was intolerable. The members of the League, who had complete control of the capital, had appealed to Spain for help. There was a real danger that the king could lose his throne. At this point, he submissively took instruction in truths of the Catholic faith, renounced Protestantism on July 25, 1593 and, in March of the following year, he was at last able to enter Paris. Even so, some members of the League remained hostile to him, secure in the knowledge that they could count on Spanish support. In 1595, Henri IV declared war on Spain and won the battle of Fontaine-Française. The Spaniards replied by seizing Cambrai and Amiens (1597). A brief campaign righted the situation; Mayenne rallied. The governor of Brittany, who had toyed with the idea of establishing an independent duchy, to his own advantage, formally conceded defeat. The entire kingdom recognized Henri IV; on April 30, 1598, he signed the famous Edict of Nantes, establishing freedom of conscience

After the assassination of Henry III, his successor Henry IV was to conquer his kingdom, as the Catholics did not want a Huguenot sovereign.

Maximilian de Béthune, Duc de Sully, was the most faithful companion of Henry IV.

and of worship, and marking the triumph of the spirit of tolerance. On May 2, the Treaty of Vervins brought peace with Spain. The Duke of Savoy, the last adversary of the king of France, formally yielded in 1601. The king of France had had the Pope declare his marriage with Marguerite de Valois null and void, on the grounds that consent had not been properly obtained. In 1600, he married Marie

de Medicis, though this new fact did not prevent this Bluebeard from keeping several mistresses, some of whom, such as Henriette d'Entragues, were to give him many a headache in the years to come.

Now that peace had at last returned to France, all that remained was to restore the health of the kingdom.

A kingdom is rebuilt

Everything had to be restored; in this huge task, the king was able to draw on the assistance of Sully, who, in 1598, had become the equivalent of Minister of Finance. In order to hire foreign troops, the king had borrowed massive sums of money. Sully managed the wealth of France as if he had been a solicitous father managing the family purse: he reduced expenditures, and increased, or created, indirect taxation (the tax on consumption, 1 *sou* in the *livre*). By the end of the reign, the debt had dropped by almost 4 million *livres,* and the minister of finance had been able to lower the land tax, or *taille,* which weighed so heavily on the peasants.

Public posts and the office of magistrate used to be bought by those wishing to fill them. Sully made them hereditary; on payment of an annual fee, the holder of the office could turn them over to a son or a nephew, as long as he had the required competence. A man named Paulet was in charge of the collection of the tax, whence the name *Paulette* which was given to it. The great families of counsellors in the Parliament, who were to play such an important role in the 17th and 18th centuries, came into being in this way. All the indirect taxes, like the *gabelle* (or salt tax) and the *aide,* were raised. Sully reorganized farming, and placed four Farmers-General in charge of all farms. He himself was passionately interested in agriculture: "Plowing and grazing are the two breasts at which France feeds", he used to say. Henri IV wanted every family to have a chicken in the pot each Sunday, a praiseworthy idea which was not to be entirely realized.

Industry was not neglected; Olivier de Serres, in a wise and perspicacious move, promoted the cultivation of the silkworm, as a way of avoiding dependence on purchases of such products abroad: 200,000 mulberry-bushes were planted in the Tuileries Gardens. The fact that men of gentle birth wore silk stockings was of particular benefit to the silk trade in the Lyon area. Commerce in general developed, roads were better maintained, and the towns were reconstructed. Paris was given various superb features such as the Place Dauphine, the Place Royale (now known as the Place Vosges), while work proceeded on the construction of the Louvre, the Tuileries and Fontainebleau. The architecture of the period combined classical sobriety and elegance.

Attempted murder and plots

Henri IV's victories had created great bitterness; not all of the wounds had yet had time to heal fully. The Catholic Church undertook to reform itself, and the king himself lent a hand by introducing into the kingdom the rules laid down by the Council of Trent. Yet he needed time and patience.

Since the birth, in September 1601, of a son (the future Louis XIII) to Marie de Medicis, the succession to the throne was assured. The queen also gave the king four other children. Yet the unrest of the past was not going to disappear overnight.

Henri IV survived many attempts on his life; sometimes the perpetrators were madmen or fanatics, while diehard members of the League were involved in several cases also. However, there was a great deal of conspiracy going on. Feeling that he had been inadequately rewarded for his services, the Maréchal de Biron, in 1602, did not hesitate to initiate talks with Spain. When the plot was discovered, Biron was executed. Two years later, the Comte d'Auvergne, with the help of the Entragues family,

This is a fine portrait of Henry IV, who tried to restore the kingdom and reconcile the French people. However, he had many enemies; this contemporary engraving shows him being assassinated, in May 1610, by Ravaillac, a fanatic.

lapsed into his old conspiratorial ways. This time, Henri IV granted a pardon, as Henriette d'Entragues, Marquise de Verneuil, had been his mistress. Lastly, in 1606, the revolt of the Duc de Bouillon culminated in the capture of Sedan by Henri IV; eventually, the king showed a noble measure of generosity, and returned Sedan to its owner.

The king's foreign policies were realistic; he tried to maintain the independence of the German princes, who were threatened by the House of Austria, while at the same time strengthening the alliance between France and the Swiss Cantons (1602), in order to hamper the relations between the Hapsburgs of Spain and those of Austria.

In 1609, Henri IV fell in love with Charlotte de Montmorency. He had her married to the Prince de Condé, who fled with his wife to the Spanish Netherlands just when the king was proposing to intervene in Germany to support the rights of the heirs of the Duc de Clèves against the Emperor. A general war seemed a distinct possibility.

However, the assassination of the king by Ravaillac, on May 14, 1610,

put an end to that threat. The question still remains as to whether Ravaillac had acted alone, or as part of a plot. Even today, Henri IV is still the most popular of the kings of France.

Louis XIII: *the beginnings*

When his father died, Louis XIII was only nine years old. The regency was conferred upon his mother, Marie de Medicis. This rather unintelligent, obstinate woman surrounded herself with Italian advisers, and, first of all, with Concini and his wife Eleonora Galigai. Acting on their advice, the

Louis XIII, the son of Henry IV, governed France with the aid of Richelieu. He succeeded in defeating the Protestants by taking La Rochelle. In this fine portrait he is shown in armor.

decided that he had had enough of the Concini. The Maréchal d'Ancre was assassinated in 1617, while on his way to the Louvre. His wife was sentenced to death and executed. Marie took refuge in her government of Anjou, where she tried to promote opposition to the king. Eventually, she became reconciled with her son.

Louis could now, at long last, reign. This intelligent, active prince—somewhat given to secrecy—was to find soon a great minister to help him in the person of Armand Jean Plessis de Richelieu.

Richelieu

Born in 1585, he had become Bishop of Lucon (Poitou) by 1606, Cardinal by 1622 and he entered the Council in 1624. He was noted for his intelligence, his strength of will, persistence and capacity for hard work. After the disappearance of the Duc de Luynes, the king's friend and close adviser, who had died in 1621, Richelieu was going to be in charge of the affairs of France for nearly twenty years.

Though he was an ambitious and proud man, Richelieu had only the greatness of the kingdom in mind. He felt that the interests of the State took precedence over all else. He was to prove inflexible, rigorous and opposed to the slightest form of indulgence.

Nevertheless, he never acted without obtaining the consent of the king. In November 1630, the Cardinal was in danger of a falling from favor, because of the hostility of Marie de Medicis. He succeeded in turning a defeat in the morning into triumph by evening, in the famous *Journée des Dupes* (Day of Dupes). Thenceforth, the Queen Mother and Gaston d'Orleans, the hotheaded brother of the king,

Queen Mother sought closer relations with Spain, and abandoned the policies of Henri IV.

The nobility was not happy. The Treasury, which had been so ably managed by Sully, who was now in retirement, was quickly drained. With no further resources to fall back on, Marie convened the Estates-General of the kingdom. The deputies of the three social orders drafted a whole list of grievances, denouncing the heavy taxation and excessive expenditures, and calling for reforms. But all to no avail. A young deputy of the clergy,

named Richelieu, sprang to the defense of the Queen.

Even though the king had now been proclaimed as having come of age, Marie continued to govern France. She concluded a marriage between her son and Anne of Austria, the daughter of the king of Spain. Theirs was not to be a happy union; and it came as something of a miracle when, in 1638, after twenty-five years, Anne produced a son, the future Louis XIV.

On the advice of his friend Henri d'Albert, Duc de Luynes, Louis XIII

Though Rubens depicts her in quite ordinary terms, Ann of Austria, daughter of the king of Spain, was a beautiful, majestic woman. Having become Queen of France, she had a poor relationship with her husband; indeed, it is a miracle that Louis XIV was born from their union. In Mazarin she found valuable support at the time of La Fronde. She was a very pious woman who did much to promote the charitable work of St. Vincent de Paul.

the town, which was vigorously defended by its Mayor, Guitton. The English seized the island of Ré, from which they were later dislodged by Toiras. Finally, on account largely of measures taken by the Cardinal himself (the construction of a dike closing the port), La Rochelle surrendered, in 1628. After a brief campaign in Languedoc, the war ended and Louis XIII signed the *Pardon of Alais,* which, while allowing the reformers freedom of worship, nonetheless restricted their privileges.

The same firm hand was applied to the nobles. At this level of society, duelling was a murderous pastime, which Richelieu decided to prohibit. As soon as it was discovered that plotting was going on against him, he struck down the ringleaders mercilessly, regardless of their social rank. Cinq-Mars, who was a friend of the king, and de Thou were both beheaded in 1642, in Lyon. Henri de Montmorency had been executed in 1632, at Toulouse. During the war with France, they had not hesitated to get in touch with Spain. In order to permanently dampen the nobility's will to resist, Richelieu gave orders for the demolition of many feudal fortresses which would not, henceforth, be able to serve as a center for resistance on the part of their owners.

This time, the nobility had really met its match. The task now confronting Richelieu and the king was the reconstruction of France; they set about it by creating, in the provinces, the post of *intendants,* or administrators, for justice, police and finance. These distinguished persons lived at the headquarters of the *généralités,* a Treasury subdivision of France at the time; they were endowed with very broad powers. These *intendants,* most of whom were members of the king's

were rendered incapable of conspiring against Louis XIII.

His domestic policy

Under the regency, the Protestants had been able to acquire considerable independence; indeed, thanks to their safe havens, they now formed a State within the State. In the eyes of Richelieu, it was inadmissible that, under a religious pretext, certain Frenchmen should be able to endanger the State by their policy of calling for aid from abroad when they felt it was necessary. In 1621, Louis XIII had been obliged to embark on a campaign against them in the south-east of France. The most independent Protestants, however, were to be found at La Rochelle, a port which could communicate easily with England. In 1627, Richelieu decided to lay siege to

gave protection to navigators who took possession of new lands in the king's name: they were Gorée, who landed in Senegal, and de France, the West Indies. Companies (for the West and East Indies) established trading posts to the exploitation of these far-off lands. All of the cardinal's policies were marked by his desire to ensure the greatness of France; this is more particularly true in his foreign policy.

The Thirty Years' War

Richelieu was anxious to fight the House of Austria, which, in the form of Spain and the Empire, threatened to attack France on several frontiers. For this purpose, he formed alliances with the German princes, Sweden and Denmark. There was certainly no shortage of pretexts for a war between the Protestant German princes and the Holy Roman Emperor. A covert form of warfare had broken out between them in 1618. Throughout this period, Richelieu was content to occupy Valteline, a small Alpine valley between France and Italy, in order to hamper communications between Spain, which was master of a part of Italy, and its Flemish possessions. He also occupied certain strategically important fortresses in Lorraine which were at the time under the control of the Holy Roman Empire.

But France's allies were dwindling away. When, in 1635, open war broke out, the kingdom did not fare very well. The Spaniards took Corbie and threatened Paris; however, in Burgundy, they failed to take Saint-Jean-de-Losne. With an army of 100,000 men, Richelieu recovered Corbie, and occupied Arras in 1640, and Perpignan and Roussillon in 1642.

When he died, on 4 December 1642, the war had not ended; but the

Council of State, were instructed to develop industry, trade, and to ensure that royal edicts were complied with. In the words of Ernest Lavisse, the *intendant* was "the king present in the provinces".

With the help of a number of reliable and hard-working advisers, such as Abel Servien or Père Joseph de Tremblay, the *"éminence grise"*, Richelieu organized the central au-

thority of the kingdom, without, however, introducing any innovations. Under him the king's councils operated with full efficiency: these were the Conseil des Dépêches, the council of finances, and, above all, the Extraordinary Council, where matters of high state were discussed.

Richelieu took a particular interest in the colonies. He encouraged the colonization of Canada and India, and

Armand de Plessis de Richelieu, whose ambition, strength of character and intelligence carried him all the way from the minor nobility of Poitou to the highest positions of power. Having become a prince of the Church and Prime Minister of Louis XIII, he was in control of French politics for nearly thirty years. He triumphed over the House of Austria in the battle of Rocroi (bottom right) which is depicted in this remarkable painting by Sauveur Le Conte.

Cardinal's essential aim, to give France a set of natural frontiers, was in the process of being achieved.

French society

During the reign of Louis XIII, the Catholic Church had undergone a profound renewal, which had been encouraged by the king, a man of almost scrupulous piety, and by Richelieu himself. The rules of the Council of Trent were more fully applied. Through the efforts of Saint Vincent de Paul, seminaries were founded for the training of priests. Cardinal de Bérulle and M. Olier, the first superior of the seminary of Saint-Sulpice in Paris, contributed to these developments, but Monsieur Vincent turned his attention more particularly towards the forgotten members of society, the sick and the poor. He helped bring about some long-overdue changes in the hospitals. Saint Vincent founded the congregation of the Sisters of Charity with the aid of Louise de Marillac. He thus protected waifs and strays while at the same time arousing the interest of the ladies of high society and even the queen herself in his work.

Gradually, the zeal and piety of the parish priests revived the religious feelings of the faithful. Together with Mabillon, the Benedictines of the Abbey of Saint-Maur laid the foundations of historical method and research. New orders were also being founded: the Oratorians, whose colleges, competing with the Jesuits, gave a more modern type of education than was provided by the older universities. Nonetheless, the Sorbonne remained powerful and authoritative.

In order to protect the purity of the language, Richelieu, who was interested in arts and letters, founded the French Academy, in 1637. A new brand of tragedy was in the making, thanks to Corneille (*Le Cid* was written in 1636). The top hostesses of high society held literary *salons*. This was an environment in which the "*précieuses*", soon to be ridiculed by Molière held sway.

Louis XIII himself did not neglect the arts. In 1624, he had acquired the property of Versailles.

The king died, a tired and sick man, at Saint-Germain-en-Laye, in 1643.

7 The Sun-King

The end of the war

When his father died, Louis XIV, who had been born in 1638, was only five years of age. Louis XIII had set up a special Regency Council, in order to reduce the power of Anne of Austria, who had been designated as regent. Anne forced the young king to hold a "bed of justice", a solemn act which obliged the magistrates of the Parliament of Paris to record the royal decisions. The last will and testament of Louis XIII had been violated: Anne of Austria governed alone, with the assistance of Cardinal de Mazarin, a sophisticated and clever man who had worked under Richelieu.

The war against Germany and Spain continued. Although Spain had not abandoned its hopes of defeating France, the Duc d'Enghien (the future Grand Condé) won splendidly at the battles of Rocroi and Turenne, and forced Bavaria to come to terms with him after the battle of Nordlingen (1645). Fighting was going to continue for another five years in Germany and Spanish Flanders, but peace negotiations had begun in 1644, and the documents known as the Westphalia Treaties were signed at Munster and Osnabruck in 1648. The House of Austria emerged from this long struggle in a very weakened state; the Three Bishoprics at last became French, and Alsace became half-French. On the other hand, the struggle with Spain was far from over—it was to go on for another eleven years.

La Fronde

These wars had cost a lot of money. As early as 1644, Mazarin and Anne of Austria had been obliged to borrow heavily and to greatly increase taxation. However, in order for financial edicts to became law, they had first to be recorded by the Parliament of Paris—which the magistrates now refused to do. Frequent "beds of justice" (so called because the king, in the Parliament, sat on a couch shaped like a bed), at which the magistrates voiced ever louder and more insistent opposition to the royal demands. The opposition movement was called La Fronde, from the French word for slingshot. Seeking to extend their political prerogatives, the magistrates pressed for reforms which they them-

Jean-Baptiste Poquelin, known more commonly as Molière, was the son of a royal tapestry-weaver. He was irresistibly drawn to the theater, and, rather than following his father's trade, he preferred to tour France with a group of actors. His plays were soon an immense success. This protégé of Louis XIV produced, within a few years, a series of comedies which lashed out at the ways of his time while nevertheless preserving a universal appeal.

selves had prepared, and which greatly limited the power of the king and of Mazarin. The Cardinal gave his name to the hostile pamphlets, or *mazarinades*, which formed part of a general campaign against him.

Anne of Austria arrested one of the more outspoken magistrates, Councillor Broussel, thereby sparking off a full-scale riot in Paris, which suddenly began to bristle with barricades. Broussel was released. At Rueil, a

grim but beaten Anne signed a declaration accepting most of the demands of the magistrates. The parliamentary Fronde, or slinging match, was over.

Another slinging match, this time between princes, was about to begin. Gaston d'Orleans, brother of Louis XIII, and his daughter, la Grande Mademoiselle, were at the center of a group seeking to wrest power from Mazarin; they were accompanied by

Condé's brother, the prince of Conti, Gondi, deputy to the Archbishop of Paris, and others. In January 1649, Anne and her children fled from Paris and went to Saint-Germain-en-Laye, a chilling trip which Louis XIV was never to forget. His dislike for the capital dated from that day. The Parisians, however, quickly lost interest in this war of the princes. The faithful Condé had laid siege to Paris, which eventually yielded. Peace was signed at Rueil in March. Anne returned to Paris, and, in January 1650, arrested the principal opposition figures, out of a desire for revenge. Disorders immediately occurred again. Bordeaux, which had rebelled, had to surrender after a two month siege.

Feeling secure in his victory, Mazarin released the princes, whereupon the Fronde started again, this time more violently than ever before. Condé, the victor of Rocroi, went back to the rebel camp. This time, it was a civil war. The insurgents had obtained the assistance of Spain, which was still in a state of conflict with France, and even of England. Mazarin had to leave France. But Louis XIV and his faithful army took Angers (February 1652), were victorious, with Turenne, at Bléneau, and marched on Paris, where Condé had retreated. By ordering the canon of the Bastille fired on the royal troops, the Grande Mademoiselle saved Condé (the Battle of the Faubourg Saint-Antoine). The Parisians themselves were increasingly weary of the whole conflict. Condé fled abroad. The others surrendered. The king returned in triumph to Paris, and Mazarin, too, returned, more powerful than ever. This absurd struggle had exhausted France, and caused enormous destruction. After the Fronde, Louis XIV was absolutely determined to

Mazarin, whom Richelieu himself had named as his successor, had to confront grave difficulties after the Cardinal's death. In this portrait the power of his gaze and the fineness of his features are particularly striking.

impose his royal authority on the princes and the nobility. The absolute monarchy was one of the consequences of the Fronde.

The end of the war with Spain

Louis XIV was solemnly crowned at Reims on 7 June 1654. At quite an early stage, he made his intentions clear by forcing the Parliament of Paris to bow to his will. While he may not have actually said: "The State is me", the king's speech to the magistrates carried very much the same message.

The Spanish war was still dragging on. Mazarin had obtained an alliance with Cromwell's England. In Italy, Casale was occupied; in Flanders, Landrecies was taken by Turenne, who, in 1658, had made a name for himself by winning the Battle of the Dunes. He seized Dunkirk, where the English were beginning to settle in, and then took Gravelines and threatened Ghent and Brussels. Louis XIV had taken part, with Mazarin, in some of these campaigns. Meanwhile, Fouquet, minister of finance, had restored the financial health of the kingdom, though the methods he used to this end were not always the most scrupulous.

The Spanish king, Philip IV, was obliged to yield. The Treaty of the Pyrenees was signed on Conference Island, in the middle of the Bidassoa (the river which separates the two countries), on September 3, 1659. France received Roussillon, Cerdagne, Artois, several towns of Spanish Flanders and the Duchy of Bar. The prince of Condé returned to favor. Louis XIV married Marie-Therese of Austria, daughter of Philip IV, at Saint-Jean-de-Luz, on June 9, 1660.

Cardinal Mazarin died on March 1661. The king announced that he intended to govern the country alone.

The Sun-King

Louis XIV was then twenty-four years of age. He was a short man (his height was about 5′1″, but his wig and high heels raised this to nearly 6 feet) with a truly majestic bearing. He was keenly aware of the importance of his role and exceedingly courteous. This hard-working, devoted man was passionately fond of his kingly function, and performed it with ceremonial and rituals which he himself devised, from one end of the day to the other. In his mind, the greatness of France and his own greatness were one and the same thing.

He loved women. Even though his wife worshipped him, he nonetheless had many mistresses: Mlle de La Valette, Mme. de Montespan who was to give him seven children who were later made legitimate. After his wife's death in 1683, the king returned to a more virtuous role with his new wife, Mme. de Maintenon, whom he married secretly.

The whole episode of the Fronde had convinced him that it was absolutely necessary to tame the nobility, and to ensure subservience by compelling them to live near to the king, in order the more easily to seek the royal favor. This is why Louis XIV built Versailles.

Versailles

In thirty years, Louis XIV turned

This painting shows the Château de Versailles before the great extensions which were to make this building one of the most prestigious monuments of France. Here we see the Marble Court, which in those days had an iron grill, and also the Ministry wings and the smaller château of Louis XIII. Versailles was the focal point of French political life in France until the Revolution. Now, the palace is a museum devoted to "all the glories of France".

his father's modest *château* into the most beautiful palace in the world. Le Notre designed the park. Le Vau (who had worked on the Louvre), D'Orbay, and then Hardin-Mansart vastly enlarged the earlier building by adding the *Galerie des Glaces*, the King's *Grands Appartements* and those of the Queen. The painter Le Brun decorated the ceilings. The greatest artists worked at Versailles. Visitors stood in wonderment at the sight of the statues, the Francine fountains and pools with bronze figures. In 1671, Louis XIV created the town of Versailles which replaced the old village. Later, he built the *Grande Ecurie* and the *Petite Ecurie*, the *Grand Commun*, where meals were prepared, *Le Trianon*, where he went to rest, and lastly the chapel, "the palace of God in the palace of the king".

The courtiers flocked to Versailles, where they remained, from dawn to dusk. A glance from the Sun-King filled them with joy. When the nobles were not away at war, which they often were, they found that they had no time for conspiracy, as Louis XIV

There are a great number of portraits of Louis XIV; this one is by Rigaud, shows the king, in all his majesty, in the middle of his reign. Although he was not a tall man (5'5''), he had an imposing, authoritative presence.

used to lay on the most lavish banquets for their benefit.

The ministers and their function

In September 1662, Louis XIV had arrested Fouquet, whose wealth (and conduct) had irritated him. Fouquet was to end his days in the citadel of Pignerol. The Sun-King (this was the emblem he had chosen as a symbol of

his majesty) had chosen as ministers ordinary members of the bourgeoisie in whom he had full confidence, and whom he was to shower with honors: Colbert, Louvois, Vauban.

Colbert, the son of a Reims draper, was an extremely hardworking man who had come to the notice of Mazarin and worked under him. He restored order in the state's finances, and introduced many new indirect taxes (tobacco, stamped paper), a move which was to give rise to a violent revolt on the part of the Breton peasants in 1675. He also, reduced the land-tax, or *taille*. He did much to promote industry by establishing large manufacturing enterprises (tapestry factories at Beauvais,

Gobelins and Saint-Gobin). He facilitated trade by the establishment of roads and canals (the Canal du Midi, built by Riquet), and, above all, by his protectionist policies (*colbertisme*), as he closed the frontiers to foreign products, thus causing the war with Holland.

Colbert developed the navy by making Brest, Rochefort and Toulon into major naval ports. At one point, the naval squadrons had 200 warships. Lastly, he encouraged settlement in the colonies and set up new trading companies.

Louvois, the Secretary of State for War, set about reorganizing the army. He compelled the officers, all of them noble, to concern themselves with

The morning was usually the time when Louis XIV granted solemn audiences to the envoys of other European nations and the foreign princes who visited him. Great emphasis was laid on the majesty of these occasions. With his wig (5½″) and his high heels (5″), the king was able to survey his guests from a commanding height. Here we see the Elector of Saxony bowing before the Sun-King, who is surrounded by ladies and courtiers.

their regiments. He restored discipline and promoted recruitment. He replaced the heavy musket by a new, lighter weapon, created stockpiles of foodstuffs and weapons and provided ambulances for the wounded.

Lastly, a word should be said about Vauban. Through his bold ideas, this military engineer revolutionized the art of fortifications, giving most of the major cities or frontier towns a new defensive system.

Thanks to these three men, and to several others besides, France became a great modern state, the most modern in Europe, and Louis XIV could embark on wars of conquest.

The first wars

The king of Spain had to pay a very large dowry to Louis XIV, and could not raise the required funds. Under the pretext of the right of succession, Louis XIV attacked the Spanish Netherlands (modern Belgium and Flanders) in 1667. Turenne occupied the area but soon ran into opposition from Holland, whose leaders were disturbed by the proximity of France and the protectionist measures adopted by Colbert. In 1668, Condé invaded the Franche-Comté. The Treaty of Aix-la-Chapelle (1668) brought peace. Louis XIV kept no part of Flanders and returned Franche-Comté.

Through his sister-in-law, the wife of King Philip, the king sought closer relations with England. But Henriette died suddenly, possibly poisoned by jealous suitors.

Louis XIV wished to punish Holland, the United Provinces which had resisted his plans. He declared war on them in 1672. At the head of his armies, the king crossed the Rhine, and took Arnhem and Utrecht; however, William of Orange opened the dikes,

flooded the countryside and effectively stopped the invasion. The French took Maestricht. England withdrew from the alliance with France, preferring instead to ally itself with the United Provinces, which also enjoyed the support of the German Empire. Condé won the battle of Seneffe; the whole of Franche-Comté was occupied. Turenne invaded the Rhineland and the Palatinate. The allies threatened Alsace; Turenne embarked upon a magnificent campaign against them in 1675, but was killed on July 7. Duquesne was victorious at sea, and Philippe d'Orleans won the battle of Cassel. In 1678, the allies, now close to exhaustion, signed the Treaty of Nimegue, which set the seal on the victory of France, ceding to it all of Flanders and Franche-Comté. The reign of the Sun-King was at its apex.

Unity and opposition

Louis XIV sought to make all Frenchmen united in spirit and faith. Literature was passing through a most brilliant phase: Racine, Molière (who died in 1672), La Fontaine and his Fables, Boileau and his *Art poétique,* La Bruyère, who in his *Les Caractères,* described life at court, or the Marquise de Sévigné, whose letters reported the gossip of Versailles—all of them were of unrivalled talent. Science and philosophy, with Pascal and Descartes, whose clear, precise reasoning brought the Cartesian method to the world, sacred eloquence with Bossuet and Fenelon: these were truly creative minds, which left behind them many immortal works.

Unity, however, was not complete. Certain recalcitrant writers would not bow to the rules of classicism. More importantly, religion began to divide men yet again. The doctrine of the

Bishop of Ypres, Jansenius, became quite widely accepted in France. He held that divine grace is denied or granted to all Christians in accordance with predestination. An austere mode of life was the logical consequence of such a doctrine. Jansenism had been adopted by men of great virtue, like the Arnauld, and had spread to certain religious houses (Port-Royal). The Jansenists were opposed to the indulgence of the Jesuits, against whom Pascal had written the *Provinciales.* Unfortunately, the dispute spilled over from the religious sphere into politics, and the Port-Royal movement eventually became so vehemently opposed to the king that Louis XIV had to disperse the nuns involved, close down their convent and destroy it. The Jansenist conflict caused a great deal of unrest in France while it lasted.

The revocation of the Edict of Nantes, and its consequences

The Protestants were bullied, persecuted, threatened and subjected to forced conversions. Partly through his inaccurate information on the true state of affairs, and partly on account of the influence of Mme. Maintenon, whom he had just married, the king, who had now returned to the piety of his earlier years, revoked the Edict of Nantes in 1685, in the belief that there were few reformers left in France. He was hopelessly wrong. The Protestants were still very numerous. Many of them fled abroad, thus depriving France of many fine minds. Others went into hiding, held clandestine meetings and confessed their faith despite executions or the prospect of being sent away as a galley-slave or ending their days in prison. Eventually, they rebelled and took up arms against the forces of the king.

The revocation of the Edict of Nantes was a grave blunder, which was to lead to the War of the League of Augsburg.

The last wars

Under the authority of its his new king, the former *stathouder* of the Netherlands, William of Orange, England was now the enemy of France. The Stuart King James II had taken refuge in France. Louis XIV occupied Strasbourg and a number of towns in Alsace, thus providing an excellent pretext for the Emperor to ally himself with the German princes, England, the Duc de Savoie and Spain, in a new coalition against the Sun-King. He could no longer count on Condé and Turenne, but the Maréchal de Luxembourg, Catinat, and, above all, Jean Bart, Duguay-Trouin, and Tourville were outstanding leaders. After some initial successes on land, (Fleurus, 1690, and Staffarde in Piemont) and at sea, the French troops occupied Nice and Piemont, but the naval defeat of La Hougue (1692) put an end to James II's hopes of returning to the throne. The Maréchal de Luxembourg and Catinat continued, however, at Neerwinden and La Marsaille; but the war had exhausted the resources of France. A tax *per capita* of the population had to be introduced: whence its French name, *capitation.*

In 1697, the Treaty of Ryswick restored the *status quo* between France and the United Provinces. Louis XIV recognized William of Orange and reinstated the trading privileges formerly enjoyed by the Dutch. He accepted the freedom of the seas. The king handed back to the Emperor the lands of occupied Alsace, with the exception of Strasbourg. But for two towns, Lorraine was given back to its

lonial empire. It was neither a victory nor a failure.

The War of the Spanish Succession

The death of Charles of Spain re-opened the whole issue. As heir, he had named the Duke of Anjou, the grandson of Louis XIV, who accepted the testament in 1700. There were no longer any Pyrenees. The coalition against the Sun-King came into being once more, and, this time, it coincided with revolt among the Protestants of the Cévennes against the persecutions to which they were subjected. Headed by Cavalier, they were to fight on for three years; the king had to divert several regiments to deal with these insurgents who continued, clandestinely, with their form of worship.

After some initial successes by Villars over the imperial troops, at Nordlingen and Höchstädt, 1703, things began to go badly for France. The Anglo-Dutch forces occupied Spanish Flanders, and, in Spain, the English took Gibraltar. French troops were defeated at Ramillies, and then at Turin, by Prince Eugene of Savoy, an outstanding general. The Duc d'Anjou, who had become Philip V of Spain, was driven from Madrid. In 1708, Prince Eugene took Lille.

The situation was serious. Taxes had been increased, and some which had once been abolished had been re-introduced under the pressure of events. The ordinary people were enduring great suffering. The winter of 1709, which was exceptionally cold, caused severe shortages. It was so cold that the wine in the carafes at Versailles froze! A large body of opinion, supported by Mme. de Maintenon, wanted peace. Yet, despite his age, Louis XIV remained calm. He agreed to start negotiations, but broke them off when as he learnt that the allies were demanding that he declare war on his own grandson. Finally, the Duc de Vendôme won the battle of Villaviciosa in Spain, while Villars won at Denain (1712), thereby saving France. The allies, tired of this long war, agreed to sign a peace at Utrecht (1713) and Rastatt. In Canada, Louis XIV ceded Acadia and Newfoundland (without fishing rights) to the English; in the Netherlands, the king abandoned Ypres, Furnes, and Tournai, but recovered Lille. He returned Nice and Savoie to the Duc de Savoie, together with Sicily (on behalf of his grandson, who also lost Gibraltar, but was universally recognized as king of Spain).

These were sad years for the king: he lost his son, the Grand Dauphin, his brother Philippe, and his grandsons the Dukes of Burgundy and Berry. All that was left to him was a great-grandson, a five year-old child who was to become Louis XV. Exhausted, but faithful to his aims, the king died at the age of 77, on September 1, 1715.

It is not easy to say whether the French were happy under Louis XIV. The peasants certainly suffered a great deal. During his later years, the king's popularity declined markedly as a result of successive devaluations of the currency, heavy taxation and various shortages. His reign had lasted too long.

8 The Age of Enlightenment

The Regency

In his will, Louis XIV had requested that government of the country should be entrusted to a council; yet, as had happened to his father's will before him, his wishes were disregarded, and the regency was given to Philippe d'Orléans, Louis XIV's nephew.

The nobility, which had been kept under strict control during his reign, now began to feel liberated. For six years, Versailles was left unattended. The Regency was a time of unbridled pleasures, of debauchery and depravity, – an area in which Philippe himself set the example.

However, the country had to be governed. France lay exhausted; the State, close to financial ruin, had had to borrow immense sums from financiers. The Regent tried to administer the kingdom with the advice of nobles who turned out to be quite incompetent. Financiers who had grown rich overnight were demanding to be paid. Eventually, he called in an ingenious Scot, John Law, who applied his own special system.

This system involved founding a bank (which soon became a State bank) which issued notes intended to replace the heavy, cumbersome metallic coins. It was a tremendous success. As backing for his notes, Law created (or took over) commercial companies in order to exploit the colonies. The shares of these companies proved to be as unreliable as the notes themselves; their prices reached extraordinary levels, yet dividends were low. The cautious investor sold his shares, the prices of which were tumbling. The notes could not be reimbursed. After a number of last-ditch efforts, the system collapsed and bankruptcy followed.

The system gave rise to an immense shuffling of fortunes; many religious communities and many nobles were ruined. But the State was able to repay a part of its debts in notes. This collapse turned the French against banknotes for many years to come.

As Secretary of State for Foreign Affairs, Cardinal Dubois practised, throughout the Regency, a policy of peace and better relations with England and the Empire. After his death and that of Philippe d'Orleans, the Duc de Bourbon occupied this post for a short while; then, Louis XV called in Cardinal de Fleury, his former tutor, as his adviser.

The king

Louis XV was very handsome, intelligent, elegant, and intensely devoted to the ideal of peace; it is hardly surprising that he became the darling

A large number of engravings recorded the wave of speculative frenzy which swept across France during the heady days of John Law, the Scottish financier who proposed a novel system to the Regent, Philippe d'Orleans. It was not uncommon for street fights to break out between people trying to get hold of shares issued by the colonial companies.

of France. His interest in matters of state certainly equalled that of his grandfather, but he was timid, sceptical and became bored quickly. He lacked willpower, and could not govern unless he had reliable advice to go on; the source of such advice was, for many years, Fleury, later the Marquise de Pompadour, and Choiseul.

Louis had married Marie Leczinska, daughter of Stanislas, the deposed king of Poland. She gave him ten children, but he soon grew tired of her, and began a long series of mistresses: the three daughters of the Marquis de Nesle, Lousie Louise de Mailly, Mme. de Vintimille, the Duchess of Chateauroux; then came the Marquise de Pompadour, who, though his mistress for only six years, remained an incomparable friend for him; also there were the little *sultanes* of the Parc-aux-Cerfs, and, finally, Mme. du Barry. This was certainly not the age of marital fidelity, though one should not exaggerate such matters.

Fleury

Cardinal Fleury was a wise, austere man, who had the best interests of the kingdom at heart. He governed prudently; his first act was the stabilization of the currency, the value of which was to remain unchanged until the Revolution; he thereby facilitated trade, business and industry.

Public opinion remained divided over certain grave problems. Jansenism was still very influential, despite the Papal Bull *Unigenitus*, which had condemned it. The clergy which was faithful to the Pope insisted that the dying declare their support for this Bull. The Parliament of Paris and the other courts, which were hostile to the government, condemned this attitude and maintained a steady opposition which Louis XV dared not suppress. The consequences of these disputes were to be felt throughout the country: they were to deter many of

the faithful from the practice of religion because of the rigidity of Jansenism; and they were to help make the 18th century the age of scepticism—though, here again, one must be careful not to exaggerate, as there were many areas, in both town and country, which remained Christian.

Fleury tried to help develop the country's agriculture; through the Administration of Bridges and Highways, which he created, he did much to ensure that roads were kept in a good state of repair. Like Louis XV, he would have preferred peace with the rest of Europe; yet he found himself drawn into two wars.

The War of the Polish Succession (1733–1738) was caused by the accession to the Polish throne of Augustus III, the son of Augustus II, who had expelled Stanislas Laczinski. As an ally of Spain and Sardinia, France intervened in order to restore the rights of the queen's father. Fighting took place in Italy and Lorraine. Finally, after the intervention of Russia, Augustus III was allowed to remain on the throne, but François II, Duke of Lorraine, abandoned the province, to become Duke of Tuscany, in favor of Stanislas; the Treaty of Vienna stipulated that Lorraine would become French once again on the death of Stanislas.

The War of the Austrian Succession was much more serious. In it, France and Prussia, its intermittent ally, were ranged against England and Austria (1740–1748). Emperor Charles VI had named his daughter Marie-Theresa and his son-in-law François II, former Duke of Lorraine, as his heirs; but his intentions were opposed by Prussia, which had designs on Silesia, and certain German princes (Saxony, Bavaria) who wanted a German emperor. Each of them wished to

weave their own design in the imperial cloak. Reluctantly, Fleury and the king were forced to intervene by the powerful anti-Austrian faction at court. Besides, England and France were coming into conflict at sea and in India and Canada; the English looked on with growing disquiet as Dupleix brought the Hindu provinces increasingly under French influence, and as France began to encircle the English possessions in North America.

The French armies advanced as far as Prague; then, despite Chevert's heroic resistance there, they were driven back to the Rhine. The English, in an alliance with the Dutch and with the help of the Hanoverians (Hanover being a patrimonial possession of the English king) were threatening the French frontiers (1744). Louis XV

went in person to accompany the armies in Flanders and then in Lorraine; the danger was averted. With the Maréchal de Saxe, he won a superb victory at the battle of Fontenoy in the following year. The Maréchal went on to even more victories, while the French also seized Savoy and Nice.

However, at in the Treaty of Aix-la-Chapelle (1748), France gave back all its conquests, and the *status quo* was restored in India and in Canada. The war had been costly in terms of men and money; in fact, it had proved necessary to introduce the *vingtième* (the twentieth part of each person's income) but the tax, which was ill-distributed and unevenly collected, gave rise to much anger, to the point where the phrase "Tu es bête comme la paix!" (you're as stupid as peace!) became a common insult at the lower levels of society.

Fleury died in 1743, without living to see the end of the war.

Philosophers and liberals

The war had not aroused a great deal of interest among French public opinion. The age of Louis XV was a period of great intellectual ferment.

In his *Esprit des Lois,* Montesquieu discussed the different types of régimes, pointing out their good and bad features. With biting irony and a lucid style, Voltaire attacked all forms of tyranny, and injustice. He campaigned for the cause of justice and liberty, and was to win the rehabilitation of men who had been unjustly condemned. His writings did much to change the thinking of his age.

Similarly, Diderot and d'Alembert, in their *Encyclopédie des Sciences,* fought sectarianism and undermined the very foundations of the monarchy. They used a subtle technique of cross-references in order to challenge traditional beliefs. At one point, the *Encyclopédie* was banned, but Mme. de Pompadour, a vigorous supporter of artists and writers, managed to have its publication authorized.

Rousseau advocated a more liberal education and made fashionable the kind of sensitivity which was to be the precursor of Romanticism.

The new thinking had aroused certain segments of public opinion. Enlightened minds called for a more liberal system of trade, and attacked the protectionism which was preventing the free circulation of goods. However, under the reign of Louis XV, there had been a distinct improvement in the French standard of living. The peasants were using their newfound wealth to buy land, while the magistrates and the members of the bourgeoisie were buying *châteaux.* Notwithstanding the obstacles placed in their path by the ancient guilds, business and industry were developing. The teaching of the Oratorians breathed new vigor into the youth of the country. The régime remained solid, but not for long—a new war was about to weaken it.

The Seven Years' War

In both India and Canada, skirmishing went on constantly between the French and the English. In Europe, Empress Marie-Theresa, worried by the ambitions of Frederick II, sought closer relations with Louis XV, through the good offices of Mme. de Pompadour, with the result that the old alliances were now reversed: Austria became the ally of France, in opposition to Prussia, its former ally (1750).

War with England promptly broke out. At first, it went well for the French. The Maréchal de Richelieu seized Minorca from the English, and French troops occupied Hanover. At Versailles, however, the king was stabbed, though not fatally, by Damiens (who later died the most horrible death for his offense). The Prince de Soubise was routed at Rossbach. The war was now going badly. In India,

despite the efforts of Bussy, successor to Dupleix, and then of Lally-Tollendal, France lost Pondichéry and its other possessions. In Canada, Montcalm's defense of Quebec and Montreal ended in failure: Canada was lost. Without adequate resources and a navy, France was just not able to help its colonies. England triumphed and Frederick II, in Germany, withstood for three whole years the combined attacks of the troops of the Empress, the Tsarina and the French generals, who were not particularly brilliant.

The Duc de Choiseul, who had become Minister for Foreign Affairs, realized that this disastrous war must be stopped; he therefore signed, in 1763, the Treaty of Paris, which officially declared that France had lost its colonies. The kingdom still kept only the Antilles and Gorée in Africa.

In the following years, Choiseul tried to strengthen the bonds between France and the Empire and Spain (the Family Pact), while at the same time rebuilding and modernizing the army and the navy. However, he was not firm enough with the magistrates of the Parliament, who remained opposed to any kind of reform, and, for having tried to lead France into a premature war, fell from favor (1770).

The Triumvirate

His successor, the Duc d'Aiguillon, Chancellor Maupeou and Abbé Terray formed the Triumvirate. D'Aiguillon struck at the root of the evil, by making the magistrates civil servants, paid by the State, thereby reducing their autonomy. He also restricted the excessively wide powers of the Parliament of Paris. Abbé Terray raised taxes and slashed expenditures. D'Aiguillon continued the task of reconstruction begun by Choiseul; he was supported in this his endeavors by Mme. du Barry, the king's last mistress.

Their efforts began to bear fruit;

This engraving shows King Louis XVI, surrounded by his family, taking refreshments in the garden. In front of the king, Queen Marie-Antoinette is seated with her second son (the future Louis XVII) on her knees. Their daughter Marie-Therese is in front of the table, and her elder brother, the first Dauphin, who was to die in 1789, is beside her. One of the king's brothers is standing, between Louis XVI and Marie-Antoinette. A touching scene, typical of the taste of that period.

but Louis XV died, unlamented, in 1774, at the age of only 64.

Louis XVI, or a case of good will

Louis XVI, who was Louis XV's grandson, was not yet twenty years old. He was generous, conscientious and hardworking, and really had the interests of his subjects at heart, but he chose some unfortunate advisers, and, on account of his myopia, was rather awkward generally. In 1770, he had married the Arch-Duchess Marie-Antoinette, daughter of Marie-Theresa of Austria. She was a pretty, elegant queen, but frivolous, headstrong and had expensive tastes. Her initial popularity among the French quickly turned to loathing.

Louis XVI's first concern was to dismiss the triumvirate and to recall the former Parliaments, which would

henceforth have all their old rights. As had happened under Louis XV, the magistrates were to block all attempts at reform.

Turgot, chosen by Louis XVI as Controller of Finance, was to try to apply these reforms to the kingdom as he had already done in the *généralité* of Limousin. He replaced the custom of forced labor, which was so unpopular among the peasants, by a cash contribution. He abolished the guilds, which were impeding the development of the economy. He eliminated internal customs barriers, thereby promoting the free circulation of grains and foodstuffs.

Yet, once he attempted to eliminate abuses in pensions, and cut back the expenses of the Court, Turgot ran into a solid wall of opposition on the part of the privileged. Louis XVI was

too weak to keep Turgot in office, so he dismissed him, and soon found himself obliged to turn to the Geneva banker Necker in order to correct the situation. The State debt was now a crushing burden; far from lightening it, Necker made things even worse by contracting a loan. His policy represented basically the line of least resistance; he published a state of accounts which revealed to the kingdom the extent of its financial mess, and then neatly disappeared from the scene.

The War of American Independence

France was still going to be victorious, however. The English colonies in North America had cast off the British yoke in 1776, and had formed the United States. Without waiting for an official invitation, La Fayette rushed to their help. Prompted by his Minister for Foreign Affairs, Vergennes, Louis XVI was soon to go to war against England. The policies of Choiseul and Saint-Germain had at last succeeded. The navy won several battles at sea and the battle of Yorktown set the seal on Britain's defeat. The Treaty of Versailles (1783) superseded part of the Treaty of Paris. The colonial trade, and the "ebony trade" (black slave traffic) benefited greatly, and the large shipowners of Nantes and Bordeaux amassed huge fortunes.

But the financial situation remained difficult. The affair of the Queen's Necklace (a fraud, prejudicial to Cardinal de Rohan, in which the queen was involved) produced an outpouring of violent pamphlets against Marie-Antoinette. Calonne made a vain attempt to launch a major programme of public works in order to provide employment for the masses. The deficit kept on rising. In 1787, the

La Fayette was the first to give enthusiastic aid to the young Republic of the United States of America. Shortly thereafter, Louis XVI recognized the new State, and France soon declared war on England, in support of the United States. La Fayette is seen here in the company of General de Rochambeau who commanded the French expeditionary force which fought on the side of the victorious Americans at the decisive battle of Yorktown.

king convened an assembly of notables which failed to agree on any serious reform. The only possibility which remained for Louis XVI was to accede to a widely held popular view and convene in 1789, the Estates-General of the kingdom.

France on the eve of the Revolution

French society was based on a tri-partite division: clergy, nobility and commons; but within these classes, there were great differences.

The upper clergy (bishops, abbots and canons) who clung to their privileges were very rich. Though most of the bishops spent more time at court than in their dioceses, it could not be said that they neglected their duties. Abbots, on the other hands, hardly ever lived in their abbeys, and were quite content to merely live off the income received by them. While new recruits into the monastic orders were declining in number, the abbeys still held vast amounts of property: seven, ten or fifteen religious sometimes lived in huge buildings. The more recent orders, such as the Oratorians, in particular, were still recruiting new members; generally speaking, their ideas were more liberal.

The lower clergy (curés, *desservants*, priests in charge of chapels, and vicars) were not rich. They had to live on the tithe and various other resources. Very often, they were influenced by Jansenism or Gallicanism, and supported the main demands of the ordinary people.

There were also profound differences among the nobility. The higher nobility residing at Versailles, the princes associated with the Duc d'Orléans and the great aristocratic land-owners readily espoused liberal and enlightened views, attacked the absolute monarchy and called for reforms.

The had applauded heartily at the *Mariage de Figaro,* by Beaumarchais, which presented them in a very critical light. Even so, they were deeply attached to their rights.

The rural nobility, consisting largely of former officers who were living on a meagre pension, lived very modestly on their land. They tried to maintain or to restore feudal rights, which they had not advocated for many years, and they sought to extract higher rents from their tenant farmers, which did not make them very popular with the peasants.

That leaves the *tiers état,* which consisted essentially of the *bourgeoisie* from the towns, merchants and large farmers, and counted among its members the liberal professions: advocates, magistrates and prosecutors. In the towns, the real power of this class of society was great, yet it enjoyed no political power. It sought

The painting reproduced below has immortalized the famous scene in which the deputies of the Tiers Etat, meeting on June 20, 1789, in the Salle du Jeu de Paume at Versailles, swore, on the urging of Bailly, not to adjourn until they had given France a Constitution and the freedoms which the French people expected of them. Thereupon, the Etats Generaux, which had been meeting since May, became transformed into a National Assembly.

vigorously to rectify this state of affairs. Its members joined the philosophical societies and Masonic lodges which were disseminating revolutionary ideas throughout society as a whole, even in the army. Disturbances took place in Rennes and Grenoble in 1788. The *tiers état* had, however, won a major concession, in that its representation at the Estates-General was to be doubled.

There were as many differences between the large farmers and the peasants, including the small farmers as there were between the upper and lower nobility. The large farmers coveted the wealth of the clergy, which they wanted for themselves, while the lower end of the rural scale simply wanted to be relieved of some of its tax burdens, especially as the poor harvest of 1788 had cost them a great deal of money and caused much bitterness. All these feelings were reflected in the list of grievances drawn up for the Estates-General. A common theme, particularly emphasized in the demands of the *tiers état,* was regular representation of the three classes, an assembly which would vote taxes and monitor expenditures, a more rigorous budget and the abolition of arbitrary decision-making in government.

The list of demands drawn up by the rural parishes called unanimously for the abolition of the *gabelle,* or salt tax, which was universally detested, a better distribution of taxes through the establishment of a land registry, and the elimination of feudal rights.

Nonetheless, almost all these lists of grievances showed considerable attachment to the king, even to the point of declaring their love for him. In 1789, France was still profoundly monarchist. Everything was going to change in a few years.

At the end of the Faubourg Saint-Antoine, the ancient fortress of the Bastille seemed to symbolize the despotism of the absolute monarchy. On July 14, 1789, the people of Paris, having first seized arms from L'Arsenal and Les Invalides stormed the citadel, which was defended by its governor, de Launay. Eventually, he had to capitulate, as 300 guards went over to the attacking forces. The Bastille had fallen.

9 The Revolution and the Empire

The Estates-General opened on May 3, 1789. The deputies for the *tiers état* made the granting of the funds which Louis XVI needed conditional on a prior vote on the reforms. The *tiers état* sought to have the deputies vote individually and not in separate votes for the separate classes (clergy, nobility, *tiers état*), thereby ensuring that it would have a majority. The king ordered the Salle des Menus Plaisirs, where the deputies were sitting, closed. The deputies of the *tiers état* assembled in the Jeu de Paume, and, in the person of Bailly, swore not to disperse until they had given the kingdom a Constitution. On June 23, Louis XVI held a solemn meeting at which he opposed this demand. The deputies of the *tiers état* refused to back down, and Mirabeau declared that it would take bayonettes to get them out of there, because they were the representatives of the people. The Estates-General thus became transformed into a national constitutive assembly. The deputies of the other two orders eventually went along with the *tiers état* and the king had to concede defeat.

Paris, however, was becoming agitated. Its citizens were concerned about the armed forces which had been sent into the capital; they acclaimed Camille Desmoulins, who raised the tricolor emblem. On July 13, the masses seized a supply of weapons from the Arsenal, and, on July 14, stormed the Bastille. They released the seven prisoners they found inside. The governor was killed. This was no mere riot, it was the Revolution.

While the national guards were being organized, alarming rumors began to circulate throughout the country. There was a real fear of reprisals. The peasants then stormed one *château* after another, burning or sacking many of them. In the midst of a great wave of fear, many nobles fled abroad. The Comte d'Artois, brother of the king, set the example. Then, on August 4, in a great sweeping gesture

of generosity, the Assembly abolished all feudal rights and sacrificed its privileges.

The people of Paris were still tense, however. Hardship was widespread, as supplies of foodstuffs became difficult to obtain and expensive. While the Assembly was beginning to discuss the future Constitution of the kingdom, and the declaration which was to precede it, unrest broke out among the people. Hearing that the officers of a regiment at Versailles had trodden underfoot the tricolor rosette, they rushed to the royal town, accompanied by La Fayette, who was in command of the national guard (5 October). They invaded the palace at dawn on October 6, and took the royal family back triumphantly to Paris. The king moved into the Tuileries and the Assembly took up quarters in the riding school of the Palace.

Shortly before, the Assembly had adopted the Declaration of Human Rights, establishing liberty, equality and fraternity for all, a document which still is the fundamental charter of France, two centuries later.

In Paris the deputies assembled in clubs, where they planned strategy and policy. The main groups were the Jacobins, of revolutionary inclination, the Cordeliers and the Feuillants.

The Constitutive Assembly did an enormous amount of work. In order to cope with the financial crisis which had proved beyond Necker's capabilities, it created what were known as the *assignats,* a form of paper money with the backing of the property of the regular clergy which had been requisitioned after the dissolution of the religious orders. The Assembly divided France into *départements.* All the old institutions Parliaments, provincial estates, *intendants*) disappeared. The administration of the départements was in the hands of elected assemblies. All civil servants were also elected. Taxation was changed and better distributed. The Constitutive Assembly lastly reorganized the Church of France, by voting to adopt the Civil

Condemned to death by a small majority of the deputies to the Convention, King Louis XVI was executed on January 21, 1793, in the morning. After receiving absolution from his confessor, abbé Edgeworth, he climbed bravely to the scaffold, where Sanson, the executioner, and his aides were waiting. This execution gave rise to a great outburst of indignation from the European monarchies and led England to declare war on France and to join forces with the Allies.

Constitution of the clergy, whereby the elected clergy was no longer under the control of the Pope. Naturally, a papal condemnation swiftly followed, though Louis XVI eventually accepted this Constitution. Many priests refused to swear their support for the new Constitution; they were hunted down and put in jail.

On July 14, 1790, the holding of Federation Day seemed to mark the reconciliation of Frenchmen.

1791, on the other hand, was a year of unrest. The Assembly, still working with its initial zeal, continued its attempts at unifying the kingdom by creating new units of measurement (the meter). But the religious conflict grew more severe. Louis XVI did not recognize the priests who had pledged loyalty to the new Civil Constitution. In order to regain his former authority, and at the same time strike a blow at the Assembly, the king decided to

By mid-1790, the Revolution seemed complete. In order to confirm the reconciliation of all Frenchmen, a great gathering of the national guard was held on July 14, 1790, the first anniversary of the fall of the Bastille.

place himself under the protection of the army which was still faithful to the monarchy. On June 21, 1791, he left Paris, but was stopped before he had gone further than Varennes, and then brought back to Paris to a chorus of popular derision. Thenceforth, he was a kept a prisoner in the Tuileries; the

French people no longer trusted him.

After one last revision of the text which they had been preparing for the past two years, the deputies then adopted the Constitution, which granted the king a suspending veto over the laws proposed by them. A new Assembly had to be elected. At long last, the deputies dispersed.

The legislative assembly

The new assembly, elected by a two-stage voting system, consisted of 400 advocates out of 700 deputies; it was dominated by the clubs (Jacobins and Feuillants). Danton, Robespierre and Brissot were the main figures.

Despite the king, the Assembly adopted severe measures against recalcitrant priests who had refused to accept the Civil Constitution, and also against the émigrés. Many of them were arrested in Paris and the provinces. Meanwhile, however, the economic crisis remained acute. Demonstrations were held in protest. At this point, the Assembly, prompted by Dumouriez, declared war on the Emperor of Austria, who was subsequently joined by the King of Prussia.

Emigration had cost the army some of its officers; almost immediately, it began to suffer a number of setbacks.

MARCHE DES MARSEILLOIS

CHANTÉE SUR DIFERANS THEATRES

Chez Frere Passage du Saumon

2
Que veut cette horde d'esclaves
De traitres de rois conjurés.
Pour qui ces ignobles entraves.
Ces fers dès long tems preparé bis
Francais pour nous ah quel outrage;
Quels transports il doit exciter
C'est nous qu'on ose méditer
De rendre a l'antique esclavage
Aux armes, Citoyens. &c.

3
Quoi, des cohortes étrangeres,
Feroient la loi dans nos foyers;
Quoi ces phalanges mercenaires
Terrasseroient nos fiers guerriers; bis
Grand Dieu par des mains enchainées
Nos fronts sous le joug se ploieroient,
De vils despotes deviendroient
Les maitres de nos destinées;
Aux armes, Citoyens. &c.

4
Tremblez tyrans et vous perfides,
L'opprobre de tous les partis
Tremblez vos projets parricides
Vont enfin recevoir leur prix, bis
Tous est soldat pour vous combattre,
S'ils tombent nos jeunes héros.
La terre en produit de nouveaux
Contre vous tous prets à se battre,
Aux armes, Citoyens. &c.

5
Français en guerriers magnanimes
Portez ou retenez vos coups;
Epargnez ces tristes victimes.
A regret s'armant contre nous, bis
Mais ces despotes sanguinaire;
Mais les complices de Bouillé.
Tous ces tigres qui sans pitié
Déchirent le sein de leur mère
Aux armes, Citoyens. &c.

6
Amour sacré de la Patrie.
Conduis soutiens nos bras vengeurs.
Liberté, liberté, chérie,
Combats avec tes défenseurs; bis
Sous nos drapeaux que la Victoire
Accoure à tes mâles accens;
Que tes ennemis expirans
Voient ton triomphe et notre gloire
Aux armes, Citoyens. &c.

On June 20, 1792, the people of Paris invaded the Tuileries and insulted Louis XVI, who had deceived them. A few weeks later, the monarchy was removed altogether; on August 10, the king and his family were locked up in the Temple.

France was invaded. Early in September, Danton allowed the people of Paris to massacre the inmates of the prisons, priests and nobles, for the most part without any kind of trial. Verdun capitulated, but Kellermann and Dumouriez won the battle of Valmy, in Champagne (September 20) and stopped the invasion. The next day, the Republic was proclaimed. The new Assembly, the Convention, came to power.

The Convention

The new Assembly, which had been elected by universal suffrage, consisted of three main groups: the Montagnards, sitting on the left, the Girondins (from the name of several deputies from La Gironde) who were more moderate, and the center or Marais, which shifted its vote from one to the other as the need arose.

Having come to power with Roland, the Girondins began the trial of the king. The discovery of a secret armory strongly suggested that Louis XVI had been in contact with enemy powers. This indecisive, but pious king, who had been condemned to death by a small majority, died a saintly death on January 21, 1793.

As a consequence, England declared war on France. Dumouriez emigrated. The compulsory recruitment of 300,000 men gave rise to a revolt in the west. The Convention had to cope with dangers from outside and from within.

After some initial successes, the Catholic and royalist army, consisting

of peasants who had taken up arms in order to defend their priests, was defeated at Nantes (July). After an attempt to take the port of Granville, it fell back towards the Loire, suffered heavy losses and was overwhelmed at Savernay in December. The war was to go on in Anjou, Vendée and, with the chouannerie, in Normandy, Brittany and Maine. Towns such as Lyon, Marseille and Toulon, which had rebelled against the dictatorship of the Assembly, were captured and sev-

erely punished. A young artillery officer by the name of Napoleon Bonaparte distinguished himself at the siege of Toulon.

The Convention sought to weed out the less enthusiastic members of the municipalities by sending representatives off on mission, within the country and also to the armed forces abroad. It also stimulated popular associations, and waged war on the Catholic faith, which was henceforth replaced by the goddess of Reason, just as the Gregorian calendar was replaced by the Republican calendar, all official acts now being recorded on the basis of the year II of the Republic.

The Girondins, who were thought to be too moderate, were outlawed. They tried, but failed, to incite the provinces to revolt. Most of them were executed.

With Robespierre and Danton, the Montagnards came to power. Marat was assassinated by Charlotte Corday. Terror swept the land: any suspect could be arrested. Three instruments of government were created: the Comité de Sûreté Générale, which controlled the police; the Tribunal Révolutionnaire, which, under the merciless public prosecutor, Fouquier-Tinville, condemned to death all the opponents of the régime. The prisons were full: Queen Marie-Antoinette, the Duc d'Orléans, Philippe Egalité, Mme. Roland and many others were guillotined.

The whole of Europe had alined itself against Republican France; but, having invaded the north, the Austrians, who had already been defeated at Jemmappes in 1792, were beaten again, this time at Fleurus. The French armies, whose officers consisted of men who had once fought for the monarchy and also new recruits, even invaded the Rhineland, for a brief

while. Thanks to Carnot, "the organizer of victory", they kept the advantage on all frontiers. In 1794, the Convention was victorious everywhere.

Robespierre, who was anxious to establish a Republic in the strictest sense of the term, violently attacked Danton and his friends who advocated moderation. Danton and his group were guillotined in March 1794. The left-wing extremists (with Hébert) suffered the same fate. Everyday, whole cartloads of the condemned left the Conciergerie. There were about 2,000 executions in Paris, and about 200,000 in France as a whole (counting the repression in Vendée, Lyon and Toulon).

Robespierre and his associates were now the sole masters of France. The worship of Reason was replaced by that of the supreme Being. But many were not happy with his way of running things: Robespierre tightened the revolutionary laws to the point where he sealed his own doom. The Assembly eventually turned aginst him. He appealed in vain to the

extreme republican sans-culottes. On the 8 and 9 Thermidor (July 1794) he and his friends were arrested and executed. The Terror was over. The prisons were opened, and the guillotine was prepared for the likes of Fouquier-Tinville, Carrier, the executioner of Nantes, and many others who had been involved in the Terror, and whose turn had now come.

The Thermidor Convention remained republican, but moderately so. It was faced with grave economic difficulties: the necessities of life were in short supply, particularly in Paris, where the black market began to operate. Food prices shot up. The assignats, or paper money, had lost much of their value; State property which had been confiscated from the émigrés could thus be acquired very cheaply, by those who had the money. The Assembly got rid of the last remaining left-wing extremists (Babeuf). An émigré landing, carried out with English support, at Quiberon, in June–July, was thwarted by Hoche; the invaders were captured and shot. The Assembly restored religious lib-

In order to replace religious ceremonies, the Convention instituted civil holidays and celebrations. Left: a parade of gardes-nationaux past a statue symbolizing Liberty. Preceding this scene chronologically, however, this touching print (below) shows Marie-Antoinette saying good-bye to her children before going to the scaffold. Allegorical scene: the queen did not see her children again after her transfer to the Conciergerie.

erty, first in the west, and later in the rest of the country, and allowed the opening of churches to Jurian priests. When victory was at long last achieved, it signed a peace treaty in April 1795 with Prussia and the United Provinces, which ceded to France the left bank of the Rhine and a part of Dutch Flanders respectively. Spain also concluded peace, leaving only England and Austria at war with France. In the fall, Pichegru and Jourdan were driven back towards Alsace. The Convention voted a new Constitution. Its members dispersed in October 1795, after proclaiming the reunion of Belgium and France.

The accomplishments of the Convention were remarkable (particularly in the sphere of education). It created the *Ecoles Centrales* (secondary schools), the *Ecole Polytechnique*, the *Ecole des Travaux Publics*.

The Directory

Under the new Constitution, there were to be two Chambers: the Conseil des Cinq-Cents and the Conseil des Anciens. A Directory of five members would hold executive power. Some of the deputies were chosen from amongst the former members of the Convention. Numerous problems had to be resolved: Hoche was given the task of religious pacification in the west. The last of the Vendéen leaders

were executed.

To cope with inflation, the Directory replaced the *assignats* which had lost much of their value, by a system of *mandats territoriaux*, though these, too, were to go down in value quite soon. War with Austria continued. At the head of the army in Italy, Bonaparte won the battles of Lodi, Arcole and Rivoli, forcing his adversaries to sign the Treaty of Campoformio (October 1797).

At home, however, difficulties were mounting. A new religious awakening coincided with a social and royalist backlash. Through their skilful propaganda, the royalists won a resounding success at the elections of

The Egyptian expedition was undertaken by Bonaparte in order to hinder British communications with the West. After landing in Egypt, the general marched quickly inland and won the battle of the Pyramids (July 21). Several days later, Admiral Nelson destroyed the French fleet in the roadsteads of Aboukir. A year later, however, in July 1799, Bonaparte scored a brilliant victory over the Turks, as shown in the painting reproduced below.

year V (1797). In order to counteract this reaction, the Directors, with army support, were obliged to stage a *coup d'état*: on 18 Fructidor, September 4, 1797, the Conseil des Cinq-Cents was purged of its more moderate members, and the elections were declared null and void in many *départements*. Those deputies who were most heavily compromised were deported. Harsh repressive measures were taken against the émigrés who had returned and against recalcitrant priests.

The majority of the members of the Assemblies was now fluctuating from right to left. In a deeply disturbed and exhausted country, there was general insecurity. Brigands—either former chouans or mere common criminals—attacked stage-coaches, town halls and even police stations. War had broken out once more. In these circumstances, in order to cut England's links to India, Napoleon decided to embark on the expedition to Egypt (1798). He won an engagement near the Pyramids, entered Cairo, but the French fleet was destroyed at Aboukir. After driving a wedge into Syrian territory, Bonaparte returned to France, where the situation was more precarious than it had ever been before. The French army had been beaten in Germany. Bonaparte did not hesitate: with the aid of the army and a number of politicians, he put an end to a régime which clearly could do nothing to bring about France's recovery. At Saint-Cloud, on 18 and 19 Brumaire (November 9/10, 1799), after a tense meeting, he seized power.

The Consulat

A new Constitution was prepared forthwith; it provided for government by three consuls, who would exercise executive power, though, in actual fact, Bonaparte ran everything himself. There were also Assemblies, but they wielded very limited legislative powers. Administration was entirely reorganized. A préfet was placed at the head of each département, representing the authority of the State. The First Consul also reorganized finan-

This famous painting by François Bouchot depicts Bonaparte at the Cinq-Cents, on the 18 Brumaire, year VIII (November 9, 1799). The useless chatter of the Assemblies could clearly be tolerated no longer. On his return from Egypt, Bonaparte appeared in the Conseil des Cinq-Cents, which had been transferred to Saint-Cloud. After some hesitation, the Assembly, prompted by its president, Lucien Bonaparte, agreed to confer full power on the general.

cial administration. He put the country's currency on a sound footing by creating the *franc de germinal an VIII,* the value of which in gold was to remain unchanged until 1914. After lengthy negotiations, the Concordat was signed between Pope Pius VII and Bonaparte. Religious peace had been restored.

The second anti-French coalition was crushed after Bonaparte's victory at Merango. The Treaty of Lunéville (1801) made the left bank of the Rhine French territory. Belgium and Piémont were annexed. France now had 120 départements. In 1802, England gave up the struggle, and signed the Treaty of Amiens.

A referendum appointed Bonaparte consul for life. Meanwhile, expansion continued, in Europe and overseas (San Domingo). The First Consul sold Louisiana to the United States. However, England was increasingly disturbed by industrial competition from France, so the struggle resumed, with English support going to the royalist movements led by Cadoudal, a former chouan, who was eventually captured. At this point, Bonaparte was contemplating founding a dynasty.

In order to wipe out the Bourbons' chances of returning to power, he had the Duc d'Enghien, a prince living in exile, kidnapped and sentenced to death. He promulgated the *Code Civil,* which is still the basis of French civil law. In May 1804, the Senate conferred on Bonaparte the dignity of Emperor. In four years, France had been pacified and regenerated.

Napoleon I

Napoleon, who had been born in 1769, at Ajaccio, the second son of Charles Bonaparte and Letizia Ramolino, attended military schools;

as an officer, he took part in a number of engagements during the Revolution. The Italian campaign demonstrated the full measure of his military genius, which must surely rank among the greatest of all time.

He was a remarkable organizer, with exceptional powers of memory and an incredible capacity for hard work; he had a clear mind, and quickly saw his way to the solutions of the most difficult problems. He was highly authoritarian, and could not bear to

David, the official painter, has left us this famous painting (below) of the coronation in Notre-Dame de Paris, December 2, 1804. All Napoleon's enemies were now under his control or unable to act against him, and France was at peace. Pope Pius VII came personally to crown the Emperor; but Napoleon himself placed the imperial crown on Josephine's head. France was entering a new era.

be contradicted; he was determined to be well served and obeyed. He was fortunate in that he had some fine generals: Berthier, Ney, Murat and many others.

Napoleon was stubborn and headstrong. He was very devoted to his family, and distributed thrones to his brothers, while marrying his sisters to princes. His choices, however, were not always good ones. He had married Joséphine Tascher de La Pagerie, the widow of a guillotined aristocrat, the Vicomte de Beauharnais. She produced no children for the Emperor.

The Empire triumphant

After his coronation at Notre-Dame in Paris, performed by Pope Pius VII, on December 2, 1804, Napoleon set about organizing an imperial court. He restored several high offices, on a strict hierarchical basis. His attempts to attract the old nobility into these posts were not always suc-

This painting by J.-F. Franque (below) shows the Empress Marie-Louise and the king of Rome. Although this is a somewhat conventional picture, the graceful gesture of the mother, as she lifts the veil under which the child is sleeping, is charming and natural. Josephine had been unable to give the Emperor an heir, so he got a divorce in order to marry an Austrian archduchess, the daughter of Emperor Francis II, who for a short while did provide for the succession to the throne.

The village of Wagram went into History on July 5 and 6, 1809. Despite numerous defeats, the members of the Coalition had not abandoned all hope of defeating the Emperor. Napoleon had been victorious at Esslingen. The Austrians, under Archduke Charles, attacked the Emperor on the Danube, in one of the bloodiest battles of the Empire. The Austrians were eventually defeated and compelled, a few days later, to seek an armistice.

cessful. He wanted to be kept informed of everything: his ministers had to provide him with statistics and clear, precise reports; his préfets and bishops had to keep him in touch with public opinion. The police were everywhere; there was strict censorship of the press. The Emperor worked actively to revive industry and trade.

In order to defeat England, he massed an army of 80,000 men at Boulogne, together with a fleet of 2,000 ships to transport them across the Channel. The defeat suffered by the French navy at Trafalgar (1805) put an end to these hopes. Napoleon then decided to turn this army against Austria, which, with Russian aid, had resumed its struggle against France.

His victory at Ulm enabled him to enter Vienna, and his resounding triumph at the battle of Austerlitz (December 2, 1805) in which he defeated the combined English and Austrian forces, smashed the coalition. Austria signed a peace treaty.

Prussia, which had declared war on France, was defeated at Iéna, and occupied. Russia alone remained. In the far corner of Germany, the Emperor defeated the Russians at Friedland and compelled Tsar Alexander I to accept his peace terms at Tilsitt. But Alexander went even further: he agreed to form an alliance with Napoleon. By the end of 1807, Napoleon was the master of Europe; France, which extended into Italy and Belgium, as well as along the left bank of

the Rhine, now had 130 départements.

England, however, continued the struggle; so, in 1806, Napoleon ordered the Continental Blockade, which was intended to close all the ports of Europe to English vessels, and prohibit all trade with her. The blockade was never fully applied, as England was the leading industrial power of the day and exported most of the colonial products, sugar in particular. Many nations, such as Spain or the Papal States, ignored the Blockade.

Napoleon had placed his brothers on thrones: Louis in Holland, Jerome in Westphalia and Joseph in Spain. Joseph encountered violent resistance on the part of the people of Spain, and Portugal allied itself with England.

having defeated the Russians in the battle of the Moskva. The burning of Moscow forced him to evacuate the city. The ghastly retreat from Russia then began; notwithstanding the heroic crossing of the Berezina, the manpower of the Great Army literally melted away.

In his absence, General Malet had tried to seize power. The conspiracy came to nothing, but it showed the fragility of the régime. There was mounting disquiet in the west, and a great increase in the number of malcontents. The French people were tired of war, and weak from the loss of so many young men. Napoleon rushed back to Paris, but soon had to leave again, as Prussia and Austria had begun troop movements. The battle of Leipzig in October 1813, ended in half-defeat for the French, who had to evacuate Germany. The Allies (Austria, Prussia and Russia) then began to invade France.

Napoleon then recovered the military genius of his earlier years; but his troops, consisting largely of young recruits, had had enough. His high-ranking officers themselves were weary of these endless wars. Despite the victories of Montmirail, and Champaubert, the Allies advanced on Paris. Recognizing his own defeat, Napoleon then abdicated at Fontainebleau, on April 4, 1814. The Allies left him with the derisory kingdom of the island of Elba. Louis XVIII ascended the throne. The Empire had collapsed.

In spite of bloody wars, and dictatorship, the French had just experienced one of the most exalting periods of their history. They were never to forget it, and the epic which was soon to become the Napoleonic legend is still immensely popular in France today.

The decline

In order to bend the Pope to his imperial will, Napoleon seized the Pontifical States and held the Pontiff himself prisoner, thereby alienating the Catholics of France. The army which he had sent to Spain had been made to surrender at Bailén, and a savage, costly war dragged on interminably.

At this point, Austria decided to take advantage of Napoleon's discomfort by breaking the peace. But the Emperor had lost none of his strategic gifts: he won a brilliant victory at Wagram (1809).

Since she had failed to give him and an heir, and as Napoleon wished to see his dynasty continue, he rejected Joséphine and the Emperor Francis of Austria agreed that Arch-Duchess Marie-Louise should become the wife of the Master of Europe. In March 1811, the King of Rome was born.

Tsar Alexander was seeking closer relations with England. He disapproved of the Continental Blockade and viewed with alarm Napoleon's projected Duchy of Warsaw. He broke the peace at Tilsitt, whereupon Napoleon assembled an army a half-million strong, the Great Army (whose members included nationalities other than French) and set off on the long march to Moscow, which he reached on September 14, 1812,

10 The Age of Revolutions

The Count of Provence, Louis XVI's brother, who had lived in exile for more than twenty years, ascended the throne under the name of Louis XVIII, the son of Louis XVI having died in 1795, probably at the Temple. The new king was a semi-impotent old man, who was, nonetheless, quite intelligent and liberal. He granted the French a constitutional charter, whereby legislative power belonged to a Chamber of Peers named by the king, and to the Chamber of Deputies elected by property suffrage; a tax of 300 frs. had to paid in order to become an elector and 1,000 francs in order to stand for election. Ministers were to be appointed and removed from office by the king; they were to monitor the implementation of laws and govern jointly with the king. The Chamber would adopt the budget and apply financial controls.

No sooner had the régime come to power than Napoleon's return from the island of Elba changed the entire situation. He rallied all his soldiers around him and swept on to Paris, which he entered on March 20, 1815. Louis XVIII had withdrawn to Ghent. In a conciliatory gesture, Napoleon granted the French greater liberties, abolished censureship; but all the Powers allied themselves against him, while unrest was brewing in western France. He had great difficulty in mustering 150,000 men. He marched on Belgium (battle of Ligny), and was overwhelmed by the English under Wellington and the Prussians under Blücher at Waterloo (June 18). The Emperor abdicated on June 22; he was deported and died on Saint Helena in 1821.

Napoleon's Hundred Days had made the situation of France even worse. Louis XVIII returned to a capital occupied by the Prussians and the Russians. The second Treaty of Paris gave France its 1789 borders; part of the country was occupied until a large sum of war damages had been paid. The royalist extremists vented a great upsurge of anger against the republicans and the royalists – the White Terror, which was particularly severe in the south. Marshal Ney was shot for having supporting Napoleon. The white flag replaced the tricolor. The University, which had unified education under the Empire, was suppressed, and teaching was placed under Church control, Catholicism being the State religion.

The triumph of the extremists was made manifest by the results of the first elections. The Duc de Richelieu pursued a sound finanial policy which succeeded in liberating France from foreign occupation, while General Gouvion Saint-Cyr reorganized the army. Thereafter, Louis XVIII preferred, in keeping with his tastes, to govern with the liberals, and Descazes relied on the left. The economic policy of Baron Louis attracted the support of a bourgeoisie which was getting rich quick. But the assassination of the Duc de Berry (the king's nephew) gave the Chamber a right-wing majority which suspended individual freedoms, tightened up the censorship and prevented the left from taking any action whatsoever. Insurgent movements were brutally repressed.

The new ministry, in which Chateaubriand was Minister for Foreign Affairs, decided to intervene in Spain on the request of King Ferdinand VII. The expedition turned out

After twenty-two years of exile, Louis XVIII, brother of Louis XVI, at last returned to France after the emperor's abdication. Here we see him being greeted by a courtier (upper left). However, Napoleon soon escaped from the island of Elba, where he was being held. The "Eagle's Flight", as it came to be called, brought him back to Les Tuileries. The Allies massed their forces against him again, and the disaster of Waterloo, June 18, 1815 (opposite, left), put an end to his Hundred Days.

After the death of Louis XVIII, his brother Charles X acceded to the throne. This limited, pious man, failed to understand the changing ideas of his age. The Revolution of 1830 forced him to flee.

to be a very simple affair, highlighted by the victory of Trocadero.

Louis XVIII died in 1824. His 67-year-old brother, Charles X, replaced him. The Chamber voted to grant former émigrés a large amount of compensation, restored the death penalty for those found guilty of sacrilege and intensified measures against the press. All of the measures taken by the new king, who was both pious and stubborn, with a heavily right-wing ministry and majority, caused resentment and unrest in the country. At the 1827 elections, the opposition won a resounding victory. A new ministry was formed, which tried to steer a middle course, between a stubborn right and an ardent left, at the very moment when Charles X, after certain diplomatic incidents, decided to dispatch a squadron against the Dey of Algiers. The king dissolved the Chamber. At the 1829 elections, the left won easily.

The Prince de Polignac, as new head of the government, had the king sign three decrees in July 1830, suppressing freedom of the press, raising the tax required to become eligible to vote and dismissed the Chamber once more. This was more than Paris could take: barricades were erected everywhere. From his residence at Saint-Cloud, Charles X could not, at first, believe that the situation was really serious. However, the national guard went over to the insurgents; the regular army was overwhelmed, and, after three days of fighting, Charles X and his family had to flee. The régime disappeared at the precise moment when the French expeditionary force was landing in Algiers and beginning the conquest of Algeria.

The Restoration period was accompanied by a major literary movement, which had a real impact on political events: Romanticism, which reached its apex in the writings of Chateaubriand, Lamartine, Musset and, above all, Victor Hugo. The battle at the first performance of *Hernani* (July 1830), over the new, more realistic style and feelings introduced into tragedy by the new school, was a fore-runner, in a sense, of the *Trois Glorieuses,* which led to the downfall of the Bourbon dynasty.

The July monarchy

If the people of Paris had hoped for the restoration of the Republic, they were cruelly disappointed. From the balcony of the Hotel de Ville, La Fayette proclaimed the Duc d'Orléans, Louis-Philippe, as Lieutenant-General of the kingdom. He was soon to become king of the French.

Louis-Philippe, the son of Philippe Egalité (who had voted for the death of his own cousin, Louis XVI) was a liberal prince well-disposed towards reform. His accession to power was the triumph of the bourgeoisie; he was, in fact, the *bourgeois king.* He married Marie-Amélie, daughter of the king of Naples, who bore him eight children, five of them sons.

The king began by revising the constitutional charter. The amount of property necessary to become an elector or to stand for election was lowered. Catholicism ceased to be the State religion; while it was not eliminated, censorship of the press was milder; the tricolor flag was re-instated. The bourgeoisie really knew where it stood with this king, who was a man of simple tastes. It was anticlerical and imbued with the ideas of Voltaire. The principal ministers were Casimir Perier, Thiers, Guizot, all of them bourgeois.

The bourgeoisie became wealthier and began to occupy the most vital posts in government and administration. Large-scale industry began to make its appearance, and further aggravated the plight of the working class. A number of revolts occurred,

particularly those at Lyon and also in other provincial areas and in Paris; but they were harshly put down. Improvements in animal husbandry and in land use brought progress to agriculture, though the peasantry scarcely benefited at all from all these advances. Also, many roads and the first railroads were built about this time.

The régime was still the target of lively opposition, from both left and right. In 1832, the Duchesse de Berry, Charles X's daughter-in-law step-daughter tried to promote an uprising in Vendée, though without success. Led by Blanqui and Louis Blanc, both republicans and socialists kept the country in an agitated state. Rebel movements had to be subdued. The king escaped with his life on many occasions.

The universities had been re-organized. The Guizot law (1835) made it compulsory for each *commune* to open a public primary school; but the State was still in sole charge of higher secondary education. Under the influence of Christian Democrats, such as Lamennais or Montalembert, a number of laws were passed, bringing long-overdue improvements in the working conditions of the people.

Louis-Philippe's foreign policy was directed towards peace and reconciliation. He wisely declined the opportunity to have one of his sons crowned King of Belgium, but agreed to have his daughter Louise marry King Leopold of Belgium. He sought better relations with England, received Queen Victoria, and concluded with her the *Entente Cordiale*, which, despite certain incidents due to British colonial policy, was to survive intact.

Under Bugeaud, Lamoricière and a number of others, the French army pressed on with the conquest of Algeria. The capture of Constantine and

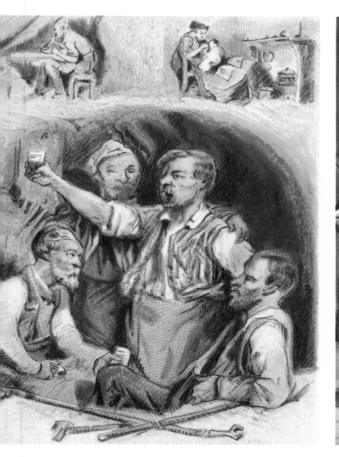

Romanticism triumphed, with its new ideas; its undisputed master was Victor Hugo. The first performance of Hernani *in 1830 heralded in a new age. The author of* Les Misérables *had waged an unceasing battle on behalf of the poor. He was the patriarch of the 19th century. In music, Hector Berlioz (bottom right) also introduced a fiery Romanticism; he also was an ardent supporter of noble causes, and his impetuous temperament led him to break with traditional dramatic art.*

The Second Empire was a period of economic change, marked by major industrial endeavors. The Suez Canal was built by Ferdinand de Lesseps and opened on November 17, 1869, by Empress Eugénie, wife of Napoleon III (top right).

Smalah D'Abd el-Kader, together with the victory of de l'Isly were the high points of a campaign which ended with the surrender of the Arab leader. In black Africa and the Indian Ocean, the government established a number of trading posts. Though not directly involved in Turkish affairs, the king wanted to seem conciliatory, and, in 1841, signed the Convention on the Straits.

In 1842, a law was passed creating the great railroad companies, which divided up the territory of France and began by linking the major cities. Protectionist customs policy lost favor, and foreign trade gained as a result.

However, the entire country was dissatisfied with foot-dragging on the part of Guizot and the king. The Democratic parties, which took their lead from Ledru-Rollin, Garnier-Page and some others, called for an expansion of the electoral law, and even for universal suffrage. A campaign of banquets began; it ended in Paris in 1848. Louis-Philippe had been able, for a while at least, to restore order, and easily upset the ambitions of Napoleon's nephew, Louis-Napoleon. Popular agitation culminated in rioting, in which the police sided with the insurgents. The July monarchy was swept away and the king had to flee. The Republic was proclaimed.

The II Republic

The Second Republic, which was proclaimed on February 28, 1848 at the Hôtel de Ville, Paris, by a caretaker government with only one worker among its members, did not assume its definitive form until the election, in April, of the Constitutive Assembly; this body, elected by universal suffrage, was, for the most part, moderate. According to the Constitution, in November, there was to be one single Chamber elected by universal suffrage, and a President of the Republic, with broad powers, also elected by universal suffrage. Prince Louis-Napoleon was elected by an enormous majority.

In order to create employment for the workers, the Assembly had created special manual jobs, the elimination of which, in June 1848, gave rise to violent rioting, which was brutally suppressed. In the legislative elections of May 1849, the law-and-order deputies won the day. But it was not long before the two branches of government, Assembly and President—both of them elected by universal suffrage—came into conflict. However, it was a conservative minister who restricted public freedom. Louis-Napoleon preferred to form a cabinet of devoted men; this was the organ which adopted the law establishing freedom of education.

Meanwhile, the royalists had agreed amongst themselves that it was time to put a king on the throne; sensing the danger, Louis-Napoleon openly denounced the helplessness of a conservative Assembly which had become unpopular with the country. His term of office expired in 1852, so, on December 2, 1851, he seized power for himself. The Republic was to last one more year; in 1852, the Second Empire was proclaimed, after a referendum which voted overwhelmingly in favor of Napoleon III.

The Second Empire

Louis-Napoleon had relied on the support of the army in his seizure of power in 1851. Now, having equipped himself with full powers, he purged the Assembly and the magistrates, the universities and the major sectors of administration. Seeking to re-assure foreign opinion, he proclaimed: "The Empire means peace". Seven million Frenchmen endorsed his policies.

Napoleon I's nephew was a very social-minded prince. He sincerely wished to do good for his people, but in his own way.

The new Constitution granted full powers to the Emperor, whose office was based on the plebiscite. The legislative body, elected by universal suffrage, adopted the budget and the laws prepared by the Council of State. He had no power of initiative as a law-maker himself: ministers were not answerable to him. The official candidacy, supported by the government, ruled out all members of the opposition, of whom there were only 7 in 1852 and 8 in 1856. The préfets and the public prosecutors found their powers greatly enhanced. The press was stifled; all that remained were several organs favorable to the government. The Orsini case (1858) made it possible to suppress the opposition even further. The 1859 amnesty put an end to this repressive policy.

The remarkable thing about this period was the amazing economic expansion which occurred in France. The Industrial Revolution had arrived: there were 12,000 miles of railroads in 1870, compared to some 2,000 in 1851; the use of machine tools and heavy steam plant increased rapidly. Agriculture, business and public works grew apace. Napoleon III surrounded himself with bankers and industrialists, and encouraged the formation of banks and lending societies. The great universal Expositions bore witness to the new wealth of France. Haussmann changed the face of Paris; the urban population grew rapidly.

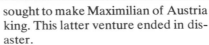

Through a number of social laws, the Emperor, who was in some ways distinctly socialist in attitudes, tried hard to improve the lot of the working class, and also that of the peasants.

During this period of the authoritarian Empire, Napoleon III, who was on good terms with England, engaged in several wars. In order to check Russia's ambitions in the Mediterranean, the Franco-British Crimean expedition, the highlight of which was the taking of Sebastopol, culminated victoriously in the Congress of Paris (1856). The influence of France now reached into the Middle East and the Balkans.

Napoleon III intervened in Italy in order to help Cavour found Italian unity (the victories of Magenta and Solferino in 1859), obtaining, in return, Nice and Savoy for France; however, he declined to intervene against the Papal States. Under the influence of Empress Eugenie, whom he had married in 1853, the Emperor then embarked on a policy of world-wide expansion: with an expedition to China, colonial expeditions to Southern Algeria, Senegal, Indo-China and, above all, to Mexico, where he sought to make Maximilian of Austria king. This latter venture ended in disaster.

The Emperor now felt that he was strong enough to liberalise his régime. He increased the powers of the legislative body, which could thenceforth discuss the budget. He granted the workers the right to strike and the right to form unions. The consequence of this latter policy was a strengthening of the opposition, whether it be Catholics who were hostile to the Emperor's Italian policies, or the industrialists who disapproved of free trade, and, in particular, the republican opposition, led by Thiers Emile Ollivier and Gambetta, at a time when the Mexican fiasco and the defeat of Austria at Sadowa (1866) had increased the power of Bismarck's Prussia. At the 1869 elections, the majority lost a million votes. The republicans, for whom Gambetta had drawn up a joint program, had 30 deputies, the monarchists 41.

Napoleon III then established a genuine parliamentary régime, granting the initiative for law-making to the legislative body, together with the right of interpellation, or questioning

Top left: Emperor Napoleon III out riding with Empress Eugenie and their son, the Imperial Prince. Right: Napoleon III restores the freedom of the Arab chieftain Abd El-Kader. Lower left: the final calamity, which put an end to the régime: escorted by two Prussian officers, the Emperor, a broken man, surrenders to the king of Prussia after the capitulation at Sedan.

of ministers on request. Thenceforth, the ministers were answerable to the Assembly, which could have them removed from office. Emile Ollivier formed the government; yet, even so, strikes became more and more frequent, thus showing the hostility of the working class to the Empire.

The new régime still had the backing of a vast majority of the population, as expressed in the plebiscite. Disaster struck in the form of a grave dispute between Prussia and France over the candidacy of a Hohenzollern to the Spanish throne; France was unable to accept such a candidate, and Emile Ollivier went to war over it, in July 1870. After the defeats of Froeschwiller and Wissembourg, Alsace was lost and Metz was in danger. The Emperor, at the head of a strong army, set off to relieve the threatened troops, whereupon he, too, was forced to surrender, at Sedan.

On September 4, 1870, the Republic was proclaimed at the Hotel de Ville, in Paris.

This imperial régime, despite its brilliant façade, was not able to survive defeat.

11 From defeat to victory

The new Government of National Defense, headed by Jules Ferry, first tried to galvanize the energy of the nation. A 300,000-strong Prussian force had laid siege to Paris. Gambetta escaped in a balloon to Tours, where he succeeded in forming several volunteer armies which tried in vain to break through the ring of troops besieging the capital. Bazaine's surrender of Metz made their efforts pointless. After a siege during which the ordinary people of Paris, particularly the working class, had suffered greatly, Paris fell. The war had ended in defeat. France had received aid from no-one; the armistice, January 1871, was followed by the Treaty of Frankfurt, whereby France ceded to the German Empire, which had just been proclaimed in the Galerie des Glaces at Versailles, both Alsace and Lorraine (with the exception of Nancy and Belfort), was obliged to pay 5 billion francs (gold) in war damages and was to be partly occupied until the end of the payment.

A national Assembly was then elected, for the most part conservative; it entrusted Thiers with the task of government. He took up office in Versailles, as did the Assembly which had at first occupied quarters in Bordeaux.

Once again, the ordinary citizens of Paris had been denied the fruits of their revolution. Rebelling against a number of ill-conceived measures, they formed a revolutionary government, the Commune, the members of which wanted to federate all the communes of France. After a fierce

struggle, the Commune was crushed, and several thousand of its members were shot or deported.

As for the form of the new régime, the Assembly was anxious to see the return of the Comte de Chambord, grandson of Charles X; but he refused to accept the tricolor, preferring instead to keep to the white flag. The attempt at a Restoration thus came to nothing. Meanwhile, by means of anticipated payments, Thiers had succeeded in obtaining the liberation of the territory. He resigned in 1873, and was replaced by the Maréchal de MacMahon. Proceeding with extreme prudence, the Assembly adopted the constitutional laws which were to serve as the foundation of the 3rd Republic, and which were to be applied flexibly and with an increasing sense of democracy.

The President of the Republic, who was elected for seven years, shared executive power with the government which was answerable to the Assemblies. He appointed the President of the Council and was empowered to dissolve the Chamber. The Chamber of Deputies was elected by universal suffrage every four years; the Senate was elected by limited suffrage, and was renewable in thirds every three years. The Council of State determined the constitutionality of laws, while the Chambers voted on laws and the budget.

The 1876 elections gave the Chamber a republican majority, whose decisions soon gave rise to a conflict between MacMahon's government and the deputies. He dissolved the Chamber. The electors returned a republican majority once again, and the President had to comply with its wishes. In 1879, he resigned and was replaced by Jules Grévy. At long last, the Assemblies moved from Versailles to Paris.

In the Chamber, there were two main parties in contention: the Opportunists, who favored spreading reforms out over the years, and the Radicals, who wanted them applied immediately. Ministerial crises occurred frequently. Even Gambetta, who had formed an important ministry, was only able to remain in office a few months. Jules Ferry was the only one who succeeded in governing France for several years, and he accomplished a great deal, as did his successors. He was responsible for several social laws, such as those concerning freedom of assembly for the public and for trade unions, the law on the press, which was very liberal in nature, the law reorganizing the departmental and cantonal administrations, and, particularly, laws making primary education public, lay and compulsory, and making secondary education available to girls.

Besides these domestic accomplishments, Jules Ferry, with the help of the army and navy, also left behind him a remarkable record of colonial expansion. In 1881, France extended its protectorate to Tunisia (Treaty of the Bardo). Following a war with China, France established a presence

103

During the bloody week in May 1871, the Communards put up a tenacious resistance against the force sent from Versailles to suppress them. The barricades had to be removed one at a time (below). Upper left: Admiral Courbet aboard his ship. This exceptionally brave sailor defeated the Chinese Black Flag force and helped the spread of the French colonial empire by extending his protectorate to Annam.

in Annam and Tonkin. In black Africa, it subdued Senegal and Sudan in ten years, and then, in 1892, took Dahomey, after a bloody expedition; meanwhile, Brazza, virtually singlehanded, had displayed exceptional skill in moving into the Congo. 1895 saw the conquest of Madagascar. Senegal, Sudan and Dahomey made up French West Africa, while the Congo formed French Equatorial Africa. Not all of these conquests were the work of Jules Ferry: many of them were the result of the efforts of his successors, who took over where he had left off. By the end of the 19th century, France thus possessed an immense colonial empire, which could not fail to excite the envy of other European nations, particularly Germany.

Quite a minor setback in Indo-China had led to the resignation of

Jules Ferry. At home, an incident on the German frontier produced a climate of tension which greatly enhanced the popularity of General Boulanger and his cause, which, for a while, enjoyed the support of a large majority of Frenchmen. However, *boulangisme* proved to be a short-lived phenomenon, and not a real threat to the Republic. The political and financial Panama scandal, however, was a real danger, especially as a number of deputies were involved.

France was now passing through a phase of economic prosperity which was given a concrete expression in the universal Expositions of 1889 (inauguration of the Eiffel Tower) and 1900. The working class did not seem to benefit very much from all this prosperity, though, and the social laws were still rather half-hearted.

Thanks to its alliance with Russia, France was now able to emerge from the isolation in which it had found itself since the defeat of 1871; moreover, there was now a better balance of power in Europe, as Germany and Austria were not the dominant powers they had once been. Delcassé, who was for many years Minister for Foreign Affairs, also did much to bring about closer relations with England, despite the Fachoda incident. A new *Entente Cordiale* was to emerge from his efforts and those of Edward VII.

At the end of the century, French opinion became divided as never before by a grave issue: the Dreyfus affair. Captain Dreyfus, a Jew, had been found guilty of spying for a foreign power and sentenced to deportation for life. Many Frenchmen found this sentence disgraceful, and demanded a re-trial. The entire right was against Dreyfus, while the left was in his favor. Eventually, the left won: after a second trial, Dreyfus was finally rehabilitated. But the legislative elections had given the Chamber a radical and socialist majority; the Socialist Party, led by Jaurès, was to pursue a violently anticlerical policy in order to punish the Catholics for the support they had given to anti-Dreyfus lobby.

The law on association (1901) closed the monasteries and convents, and sent their members into exile. Private primary schools had to become secularized and become open to all. France had broken off diplomatic relations with the Vatican and Aristide Briand passed a law effectively separating Church and State; Pope Pius X promptly condemned the new law. Violent agitation swept the country when the inventory of Church furniture was drawn up. Minister Clémenceau gradually restored calm,

105

The conditions of the working class had not improved at the beginning of the Third Republic, and strikes took place with increasing frequency. Here we see the mine workers on strike, 1880 (below). Both men and women took part in mass demonstrations which were harshly repressed by the mounted gendarmerie. It was not until a Ministry of Labor was set up that there was any improvement in the situation of the working masses. In 1914 much remained to be done.

Found guilty of treason by a court-martial, Alfred Dreyfus, a Jewish army captain, had been deported to Devil's Island in Guyana. However, many parties were convinced he was innocent and demanded a re-trial. The Dreyfus affair caused a vast amount of discord in France for five years. Eventually Dreyfus was acquitted and rehabilitated. This illustration is an allegorical print showing the prisoner, with a ball attached to his foot, waiting for justice.

while, at the same time, trying to clamp down on the anarchists who had greatly increased their violent attacks, which ranged from the assassination of the President of the Republic Sadi Carnot, at Lyon, in 1895, to the exploits of the Bonnot gang.

A return to calm was indeed long overdue; it was now urgently necessary that the patriotic sentiments championed by Déroulede or Maurice Barres should alert Frenchmen to the dangers of a new war. In 1905, Wilhelm II, Emperor of Germany, had made a threatening speech in Tangiers, in which he had denounced French influence in Morocco. War was narrowly averted, and Delcassé had to go, as the price to be paid for peace.

But the Conference of Algeciras, at which even the United States took part, finally ruled in France's favor, and accorded it police rights and commercial facilities in Morocco.

The legislative elections of 1906 had returned a left wing majority, as before. The new President of the Republic, Armand Fallières, the successor of Loubet, called for national union. However, despite the creation of a Ministry of Labor, the working classes received scant benefits. Strikes broke out in increasing numbers; Aristide Briand, despite his socialist past, did not hesitate to mobilize the nation's railroad workers to prevent them from going on strike. The law on workers' and peasants' retirement

pensions was not implemented. The wine-growers of the south mounted a powerful protest movement, which, in 1907, gave rise to some particularly violent incidents.

The 1910 elections returned a center-left majority in the Chamber. A year later, the incident of Agadir occurred. The German Emperor had sent a gunboat, the *Panther*, to the roadsteads off the south of Morocco. War seemed imminent, and not for the first time. Caillaux succeeded in holding direct negotiations, and, by granting Germany broad concessions in black Africa, managed to save the peace. Nonetheless, French public opinion believed more and more firmly that war was

AFFAIRE DREYFUS – LE PRISONNIER

This photograph shows a scene which occurred hundreds of times in early August 1914: the departure of a regiment for the front. The soldiers are confident, resolute; the women are crying and tossing flowers to them. How many of those young men were never to return? How many of them realized that this war, which had been imposed on France, would not end until four ghastly years later?

now inevitable; and, despite the persistent efforts of the Socialist party and Jaurès, preparations for war began. A law was passed raising the length of military service to three years. A Lorraine patriot, Raymond Poincaré, was elected President of the Republic in 1913. Large segments of French opinion were not willing to believe that war would come, at the end of the "Belle Epoque", during which they had considered themselves to be so happy. The war in the Balkans, which had shown the superiority of certain French weapons (the 75), and trust in the allies of France, gave them some cause for hope.

The incident, at Sarajevo, in Bosnia, on 28 June 28, 1914, in which Arch-Duke Franz-Ferdinand of Austria and his wife, were assassinated by a Serbian student, followed by the German declaration of war on France, after the mobilization of Russia and the entry into the war of Austria against Serbia, were to shatter those hopes. Jaurès was assassinated. General mobilization was ordered in France. This really was war.

The First World War and France

The weight of the First World War was to fall heavily on France. Its armed forces were roughly the equivalent of Germany's, though Germany had a clear advantage in heavy artillery. Schlieffen's plan involved a German thrust into the north of France through Belgium. French Plan XVII, applied by General Joffre, consisted of a generalized attack through Alsace. This offensive was quickly blunted, however. The violation of Belgian neutrality—a mere "scrap of paper", in the German Chancellor's words—brought Great Britain into the war, with its naval supremacy. The frontier battle at Char-

Together with Marshals Joffre, Foch and Pétain, Marshal Lyautey was one of the great military leaders of the First World War. Before the war, he had already distinguished himself in Morocco, where he had done much to enhance the position of France. After the end of hostilities, Lyautey continued his efforts at renewal and modernisation in Morocco, with the distinct aim of leading that country one day to independence.

leroi went badly for France. Belgium was entirely occupied in a matter of weeks and the German divisions swept on towards Paris.

Joffre had ordered a general retreat, with the result that, in three weeks, the French armies were brought back behind the defensive base around the capital, organized by Gallieni. The government had been obliged to fall back to Bordeaux. Meanwhile, in the east, the Germans were stopped by the Castelnau's victory at Grand-Couronné de Nancy, while Sarrail held Verdun.

In order to force the French army into a retreat, the armies of Von Klück and von Bülow turned their advance towards the south-east. Moving forward in a spearhead, however, they were in danger of being caught in a trap. The German High Command realized the danger. Joffre launched his great offensive on the Marne and

the Ourcq. After several days of fierce fighting (September 7–11), the Germans had to retreat a hundred and sixty miles and take up positions along the Aisne. The victory of the Marne had saved Paris, and, indeed, France.

The next stage was the race to the sea. Each army tried to turn its adversaries' flank by rushing northwards, to the sea. After savage fighting at Ypres, the front became stabilized from Belgium to Vosges, in an enormous arc, the center of which was at Noyon. The rich northern *départements* were all in German hands.

In 1915, Joffre attempted two major offensives in Champagne and Artois. Despite huge losses of manpower, these offensives produced the most meager results. Having stopped the Russian offensive against eastern Prussia (the victory of Hindenburg at Tannenberg), the Germans were the masters of the eastern front. But Italy

During the first seven months of 1918, the Germans had committed all their troops in the hope of a quick victory; but the failure of their last offensive in Champagne marked the end of their hopes. The Allies promptly counter-attacked and advanced steadily until the Armistice (above). Then, on July 14, 1919, there was a moving and magnificent victory parade with the participation of all the Allies. Below: Marshals Foch and Joffre at the head of the French armies.

came into the war on the side of the Allies, forcing Austria to open a new front, at the time of the unsuccessful Anglo-French expedition against the Dardanelles and Turkey, which had been an ally of Germany since 1914. Only Salonika was occupied.

In February 1916, the Germans launched a gigantic attack against Verdun in order to shatter French morale and force the collapse of the French army which, at this part of the front, stood alone against them. The unswerving willpower of Pétain, who established the *Voie sacrée* (sacred path) in order to get supplies through to his troops, caused the failure of this project. The Germans seized the forts of Douaumont and Vaux. After heavy fighting, in which 500,000 men were killed or reported missing in action,—over a few yards of ground—they had to abandon their plan. Verdun was a great French victory.

Joffre had been in command for two years now, and was thoroughly exhausted; therefore, by the workings of politics, he was replaced by Nivelle in late 1916. In April 1917, the new Commander launched a major offensive on the Chemin des Dames, in Champagne; the Germans, however, had deliberately shortened their front line. The offensive proved costly and pointless, and was stopped after a few days, but not before it had undermined the army's morale. A number of attempts to bring the war to a neutral conclusion, with neither victors nor vanquished, had already done nothing to improve its ardor. Rumors abounded. Despite the censorship, defeatist reporters were to be found everywhere. Mutinies occurred in a number of regiments. Pétain, who had been made Commander in Chief, saved the situation by certain measures which restored the confidence of the rank-and-file. On the domestic scene, disturbing events were taking place. The uncertainty and weakness of the already lifeless ministers were further heightened by cases of espionage involving politicians. At this point, Poincaré called in Clémenceau. The *Tigre* (tiger) as he was called, had only one policy: make war, particularly now that Russia, after the October Revolution, had withdrawn from the war, thereby releasing several hundred German divisions which were promptly shifted to the western front. It is true that the United States had declared war on Germany in April 1917, and that the American troops of General Pershing were beginning to land in France.

In March 1918, the German launched a first offensive at Amiens, breaking through the Anglo-French front. The Allies then conferred the High Command on Foch alone. He stopped the first offensive, but a pocket had been created. A second pocket was formed when the Germans attacked towards Paris and the Marne, in May. Foch succeeded in halting this thrust and the third German offensive was brought to a standstill in a mere three days (July).

The German army was now exhausted, and it was Foch's turn to attack on all fronts. All the German fortifications collapsed, one after another. The Germans retreated, abandoning the north and Belgium. Germany called for an armistice and, in order to obtain it, accepted the fourteen points elaborated by President Wilson of the United States. A revolution broke out in Germany and the Kaiser fled. Austria had laid down its arms. The armistice was signed at Rethondes on November 11, 1918. Victory had come at last.

12 The contemporary period

The "Mad Years"

The peace treaty which was signed in the Galerie des Glaces at Versailles, on June 28, 1919, handed back to France the territories of Alsace and Lorraine, allowed France to occupy the left bank of the Rhine for fifteen years, conferred upon it the administration of the Sarre, together with a part of the German colonies and a mandate over Syria. The question of reparations, however, was not settled, and France could not feel safe from a new attack.

The country was victorious, but it had been bled white by the war, having lost 1,500,000 men. Its economic

potential had been greatly reduced. The invaded regions all had to be rebuilt. Food prices shot up and inflation was an ever-present danger. Even so, having emerged from such grief and disaster, the French could think only of pleasure and amusement. The *post-war* years were known as the *années folles* ("mad years"), and were characterized by the frenzied pursuit of pleasure. In painting, Cubism triumphed over other forms. New literary talents made their appearance.

In November 1919, the legislative elections had returned a Chamber containing moderate deputies, whose good will did not always, alone, suffice. Poincaré had been replaced by Deschanel, who, when taken ill, was succeeded by Millerand. On his return to private business, Poincaré pressed for the occupation of the Ruhr, in order to obtain war reparations—a mistaken policy, which produced no results. The left became re-organized: at the Tours congress, the Communists broke away from the SFIO (Socialists), which then formed an alliance with the radicals forming the Left-wing Cartel which won the 1924 elections.

Herriot had to cope with numerous financial and economic difficulties. The south of Morocco had to be subdued, after the revolt led by Abd el-Krim (the Rif War); and military action was needed in Syria against the Druzes. The value of the franc was fast dwindling. Religious conflicts, which were exploited by the left, caused divisions in French public opinion. In 1926, there was a real danger of bankruptcy. At this point, Herriot and Poincaré formed a cabinet of national union, which rectified the situation.

Meanwhile, Briand, as Minister for Foreign Affairs, was calling for reconciliation with Germany (the Locarno Treaty) and voicing confidence in the League of Nations. The Kellogg-Briand Pact declared war to be unlawful.

The 1928 elections produced a center-left majority; on account of ill-health Poincaré resigned, and was replaced by André Tardieu, who continued his policies.

The dark years

The economic crisis which had struck the whole world was weakening France. In Germany, Hitler continued his rise to power. In order to achieve security against future attacks, War

Between the two wars, the French left was directed by Léon Blum, a sophisticated, cultivated man who had been leader of the Socialist party since the death of Jaures (lower left). The bloody riots in February 1934 led to the formation of the Popular Front, comprising the Socialists, the Communists and the Radicals. Many parades and demonstrations took place in Paris in 1935 and 1936 (below).

Minister Maginot built a fortified line which bore his name. In keeping with its earlier commitments, France evacuated the Rhineland and, in 1935, the Sarre became German once more, after a plebiscite.

Tardieu tried in vain to organize major public works projects, as a way of reducing unemployment. In 1932, the left, with Daladier, Chautemps and with the support of Blum, returned to power. President Doumer, who had replaced Doumergue (himself the successor of Millerand), was assassinated in 1932. Albert Lebrun then became President.

A major political and financial scandal—the Stavisky affair—involving several left-wing figures, had political repercussions. Right-wing, or extreme right-wing leagues (*Action française monarchiste, Jeunesses patriotes*), veterans' leagues such as the *Croix de Feu* (Cross of Fire), were vehemently opposed to such corruption. Demonstrations eventually gave way to action, on February 6, 1934, when a whole evening of full-scale rioting occurred, with 20 people killed and many more wounded. The Daladier government resigned. Lebrun appealed to Doumergue, who, with Pétain, formed a cabinet of national union; this time, it was the left-wing parties that started demonstrating; again, there were many casualties. Doumergue failed to reform a Constitution which did not give enough authority to the executive branch. The economic crisis deepened; the number of unemployed passed the million mark; while Hitler was seizing power in Germany, the left-wing parties (Communists with Thorez, Socialists with Léon Blum, radicals with Daladier) formed the Popular Front. Pierre Laval's economic policies had the effect of heightening the discontent in the country. In the 1936 elections the Popular Front was victorious.

The Popular Front had been victorious in the 1936 elections. Léon Blum came to power and enacted some important social measures for the benefit of the working class. The unity of the left was soon shattered by the financial crisis and external difficulties. Hitler's Germany was becoming threatening. In 1938, it was thought that war was inevitable: The Munich agreements, signed by Hitler, Mussolini, Daladier (right) and Chamberlain, saved the peace for a time.

In order to ensure that their program was implemented, the workers staged sit-down strikes. In a few days, Léon Blum, the new leader of the government, had some major social laws adopted: the 40-hour week, paid vacations, nationalization of the railroads and of certain banks. Yet the strikes continued, at the precise moment when Hitler's Germany was assuming threatening postures. The Exhibition of Art and Technology, in 1937, was not the success it was intended to be. There was still much unemployment, and, when France should have been busily re-arming, industry was stagnating. Eventually, the Popular Front collapsed; it was replaced by cabinets of union which lacked authority. In 1938, Hitler, who had forcibly re-occupied the Rhineland, threatened Czechoslovakia, by insisting on the return to Germany of

After the occupation of France in June 1940, Marshal Pétain became the head of a shrunken State. He hoped—in vain—to safeguard the country's independence. Here he is being received by a delegation of young farm-workers (below).

the Sudetenland. For the sake of peace, Daladier and Chamberlain signed the Munich Agreements, in September, thereby marking the triumph of the Rome-Berlin Axis and sacrificing Czechoslovakia, which, after the merger of Austria and Germany, the *Anschluss,* was to be wiped off the map of Europe in April 1939. But this was only a truce. Next, Hitler wanted Danzig from Poland: this time England and France refused to yield. The signing of the German-Soviet Pact of August 1939 brought matters to a head. The German armies swept into Poland, and France and England declared war on Germany.

The Second World War

The fate of Poland was decided, in a matter of weeks, by German and Soviet arms. For the next few months, the opposing armies simply stood facing each other, the Maginot Line against the Siegfried Line. In April 1940, Germany invaded Denmark and Norway. On May 11, the German armored divisions thrust into Belgium and Holland; various Franco-British divisions tried to help these two countries, while other German divisions broke through the French lines between Sedan and Namur and then headed swiftly for the sea, despite French counter-attacks around Laon and Amiens. Belgium and Holland surrendered. The divisions in the north were now surrounded near Dunkirk; the British divisions and some French divisions managed to get away by sea, while the rest were made prisoner.

General Weygand, a former adjutant of Foch, replaced General Gamelin, but it was too late. A new offensive took the Germans as far as the Seine and then on to the Loire. Despite the warnings of Colonel de Gaulle, as early as 1935, France was cruelly short of tanks; aircraft were also in short supply. The Germans entered Paris on June 14, 1940. Millions of refugees streaming along the roads were attacked by the Luftwaffe and further impeded the movement of troops. Notwithstanding heroic resistance, the war had been lost. Moreover, Fascist Italy had declared war on France on June 9, and had begun operations in the Alps. Marshal Pétain, who had succeeded Paul Reynaud at the head of the government, now removed to Bordeaux, called for an armistice, which was signed at Rethondes on June 24. Germany had taken 1,400,000 prisoners.

Occupation and Liberation

The terms of the armistice were harsh: two-thirds of France was to be occupied, with a demarcation line cutting it in two, and even in three, as

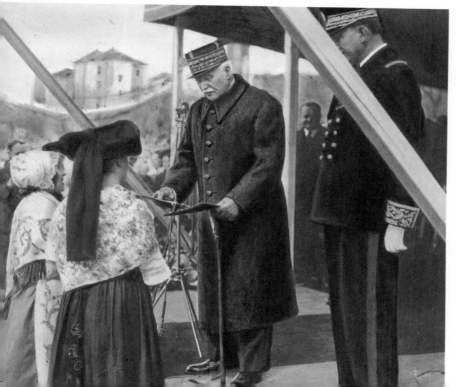

117

Many Frenchmen refused to accept defeat and joined the resistance movements. Inspired by General de Gaulle who, from London, led the Free French, they thus took part in the battle by making hit-and-run raids against enemy transport lines and by transmitting information. Here a group of members of the resistance, being led away by a German soldier.

there was a prohibited zone along the coasts and frontiers. But it was to keep a government, to be set up at Vichy, and it did not have to surrender its fleet. The Chamber and the Senate, meeting at Vichy, acceded to Laval's request that full powers be granted to Marshal Pétain to prepare a new Constitution. Albert Lebrun resigned; it was the end of the 3rd Republic.

England, however, was still actively at war; from London, General de Gaulle, who had belonged to the Reynaud government, issued an ap-

peal to Frenchmen on June 18: "France has lost a battle, but has not lost the war".

As early as the summer of 1940, several colonies of equatorial Africa joined the Free French. However, the British navy had destroyed a part of the French fleet at Mers-El-Kebir, thereby embittering French public opinion, which was already stricken by the disaster, and turning it against the British and towards the Vichy government, headed by Pétain and Laval. The French State's motto was: Work, Family, Country. It sought to regene-

rate France, but had to accede to the wishes of the occupying power. Pétain, whose sole desire was to alleviate the sufferings of Frenchmen, and obtain the release of prisoners, agreed to meet Hitler at Montoire (October 1940), and announced the policy of collaboration, which cost him the support of many Frenchmen. The Resistance made its appearance. However, feeling that Laval was taking collaboration too far, Pétain split with him in December, to the immense displeasure of the Germans and to a chorus of rage from the Paris press

which was entirely in the pay of the occupying power. In 1941, while de Gaulle, from London, was organizing the Fighting French, whose troops were beginning to fight on the battlefields of Africa, Vichy was pursuing a policy of foot-dragging. In June, a fratricidal clash occurred between a force consisting of British and Free French troops and troops faithful to Vichy in Syria, which Germany wished to occupy. The Vichy force was defeated. At about that time, Germany invaded the USSR, thereby driving into the ranks of the Resistance all the French Communists, who were to prove valiant members of the movement. At the end of the year, Germany, Italy and Japan declared war on the United States.

1942: the Resistance in France became intensified, and struck ever more frequently at the occupying power. At the same time, the sufferings of the French people were aggravated, and the black market was rampant. Laval returned to power and pursued his policy of collaboration with ever more determination, while simultaneously trying to resist Hitler's demands. He created the notion of the *relève*, which meant that, for every three French workers working in Germany, one prisoner would be released; his initiative was only a partial success. In North Africa, the battle of Bir Hakeim (May 1942) showed the world that the army of Free France had recovered its old valor. In France, harsher measures were taken against the Jews, many of whom were deported.

In November, the Allies landed in Algeria and Morocco. The Germans invaded the so-called Free Zone. The French fleet scuttled itself at Toulon. Now, the whole of France was occupied, but the number of Resistance movements grew constantly. The clandestine press began to operate.

In 1943, after heavy fighting, Tunisia was liberated. The column of General Leclerc, which had set out from the Fezzan, met the Allies at Tripoli. After some difficulties, de Gaulle became the sole leader of the Free French. Within a short while, he was to establish a provisional government at Algiers with a consultative assembly. Mussolini fell from power. Corsica was liberated. The notion of the *relève* was succeeded by compulsory forced labor, which promptly caused the disappearance of thousands of young men who fled underground, to the *maquis*. These *maquis*, which had been formed into the French Forces of the Interior (FFI), engaged the Germans in full-scale battles in 1944 (Plateau des Glières, Vercors). The Germans took their revenge by burning entire villages to the ground, together with their inhabitants (Oradour-sur-Glane). Allied bombing raids over France caused thousands of victims.

The Laval government hardened its position towards the resistance fighters, who were tortured, shot or deported. The Resistance movements merged, and a Committee of National Liberation was formed, under Jean Moulin, who was, however, soon arrested and executed.

While the French army was participating in the liberation of Italy (Monte Cassino), the Allies landed in Normandy on June 6. After the capture of Cherbourg and Caen, the Avranches spearhead made it possible to liberate Brittany and the west. Leclerc's 2nd armored division struck out towards Paris which rose up and harassed the last of the occupying forces. The 1st French army landed in Provence and moved north. From the August 15 to 25, fighting went on in Paris, where the Germans surrendered. De Gaulle entered the city on August 25. The war went on until the liberation of Lorraine and Alsace. The French army pursued the retreating Germans as far as the Danube. On May 8, 1945, Germany capitulated. Meanwhile, almost everything in France—towns, bridges, roads, railroads—had been destroyed and had to be rebuilt; Paris, luckily, had received relatively little damage.

The 4th Republic

A provisional government presided over by General de Gaulle had been formed, with the participation of the Communists. Quite soon, de Gaulle ran into stiff opposition from the Assembly and preferred to resign (January 1946). A Constitutive Assembly was elected. Despite some difficulties, it eventually drafted a Constitution which was adopted by referendum (October).

Profound divisions still existed in French society. The purging of the collaborators, the sentences passed on them (several thousands were condemned to death), the condemnation to death of Pétain (who was pardoned by de Gaulle), and a similar sentence passed on Laval, all caused a great deal of unrest. Essential supplies were hard to get; reconstruction was slow.

Under the new Constitution, there was to be a President of the Republic, with no powers, a National Assembly, elected by universal suffrage (now extended to women), which was to have full powers, and a Council of the Republic (former Senate), a mere deliberative body; decision-making power would be vested in the Assembly. Power was to be shared among three main parties: the Popular Republicans (with Bidault), the Socialists

Despite the "Atlantic Wall", the Allies, under General Eisenhower, landed on the beaches of Normandy on June 6, 1944. The assault on "fortress Europe" had begun. By the evening of June 6 a solid beachhead had been established; it expanded in the following days. The Avranches breakthrough enabled the Allies to move quickly ahead.
Here we see the first troops landing with their equipment.

(Blum and Mollet) and the Communists (Thorez). The latter party was dismissed from the government quite early on. Precisely when a strong executive was most badly needed, ministries were changing hands with monotonous regularity.

France had not been allowed to take part in the decisions of the Yalta Conference, which had divided Europe into spheres of influence. While it did participate in the occupation of a part of defeated Germany and Berlin, its voice was scarcely heard to be heard in the UN (United Nations). France joined NATO (North Atlantic Treaty Organization, for the defense of Europe) and the Marshall Plan for the economic reconstruction of Europe. Its recovery was gradual.

Yet the parties continued to fight amongst themselves. Hoping to offer

the French a new form of union, de Gaulle founded the RPF (Rassemblement du Peuple Français) which, for a while, was highly successful, and then collapsed.

Quite apart from anything else, France had to fight in Indo-China, against the Viet-minh. During the Second World War, Indo-China had been entirely occupied by the Japanese. The independence movement, headed by the Viet-minh, supported by the People's Republic of China, kept the country in a state of violent agitation. This was to be a long, painful war of attrition, lasting from 1947 to 1954. Despite the efforts of General de Lattre, France had to abandon the struggle after the defeat of Dien-Bien-Phu (1954). When the Geneva Agreements had been adopted, France withdrew from Indo-China. It

had granted independence to Syria, and would later do the same to Bourguiba's Tunisia and to Morocco, after bloody incidents and many difficulties. The tireless efforts of Robert Schuman had, however, culminated in the creation of the European Coal and Steel Community, and, later, through a series of Treaties (Rome, Brussels) in the gradual establishment of an economic (if not political) Europe, in which France could find its place.

The country's recovery was slow. Notwithstanding the efforts of Antoine Pinay, France was still in a real financial mess. The country had taken part in the Cold War against the USSR, and the Korean War. In 1956, it reacted to the nationalization of the Suez Canal by intervening in Egypt, together with an English force. Soviet and American pressure compelled

Paris had risen against the occupying power in August, and barricades were being erected in the streets. The arrival of the first armored units of General Leclerc's division (below) met with a deliriously joyful welcome. Marshal Petain was tried for treason a year later, sentenced to death and promptly pardoned. He died on the island of Yeu, in a fortress which he left only a few days before his death.

them to put an end to this expedition, which ended in failure. Worse still, Algeria had been rocked by severe domestic turmoil, since 1954. With the support of Tunisia, Morocco and the Arab countries, the Algerian National Liberation Front harassed the settlers and committed numerous attacks. The army had to intervene, often brutally, thereby giving rise to protests at the UN.

Executive power in France was weak and unstable: there had been 17 governments in 13 years! The Presidents of the Republic, Vincent Auriol and René Coty, had only the illusion of power. The legislative elections produced deputies who varied from moderate to left-wing, with no solid majority emerging in either direction. Reformers, such as the Poujade movement (businessmen) could not

sustain their initial impact. In 1958, the situation was fast getting out of hand. The French in Algeria, with the support of the army, rebelled against the impotence of the Metropolis, and threatened to take matters into their own hands, as indeed they had begun to do in Algeria itself.

In these circumstances, René Coty turned to General de Gaulle, who agreed to return to politics and was given full authority, in May–June 1958, to create a new Republic.

The 5th Republic

After a visit to Algeria, during which he tried to restore calm, while at the same time avoiding making any commitments about its future, de Gaulle drafted a new Constitution which was approved by an enormous majority in a referendum. The Pres-

Below: Charles de Gaulle, who was elected President of the renewed Republic in 1958, conducted the affairs of France for more than ten years. He wished to make France strong, prosperous and independent; yet he was unable to prevent the popular explosion of May 1968 (bottom) which was caused by discontent among the working classes and the anxiety of the students about their future. After a month of rioting and unrest, calm was restored in France.

ident of the Republic, who had considerable powers, chose the Prime Minister. Those of the National Assembly were very limited, and its sessions were made shorter. The deputies could not force the government to resign unless the government itself were to raise a motion of confidence (which would happen quite rarely), or if a majority were to vote pass a motion of censure. The result was great governmental stability. A Constitutional Council was to monitor various applications of the Constitution.

After the legislative elections which returned an impressive majority of Gaullists to the Assembly, General de Gaulle was elected President of the Republic on December 21, 1958, and Michel Debré formed the government. De Gaulle's first concern was to put an end to the conflict in Algeria and to hasten the country's financial and economic recovery. After it had been devalued, the franc became stable, and a new franc was created

(one NF or new franc was worth 100 old francs). The French economy did recover, and embarked on a period of great expansion.

After endless difficulties and vicissitudes, and a number of conferences, at a time when the situation in Algeria had degenerated into civil war, the Evian Agreements of 1962 granted independence to the FLN. All the colonies of black Africa had also obtained independence, while establishing good relations with the former colonial power. Almost all the Europeans had to leave Algeria.

While not hostile to Europe, de Gaulle made only half-hearted moves towards the goal of European union. He always opposed the entry of Great Britain into the Common Market. He resented the idea that French forces could be under foreign command in an international organization (NATO), and, while not violating the North Atlantic Treaty, he nonetheless withdrew France from the Organization. He did, however, press for the manufacture of French nuclear weapons. France became a nuclear power.

After Debré had left the government and Pompidou had been removed from office by the deputies, and after the Assembly had been dissolved and a new one elected, de Gaulle held a referendum which decided that, thenceforth, the President of the Republic should be elected by universal suffrage. In 1965, he was re-elected, on the second ballot. New economic difficulties were waiting to be confronted: as expansion had been of little benefit to the working class, there was growing unrest. Strikes became more frequent. In 1967, the Gaullist majority elected when the Assembly was up for re-election scraped in by only a few votes. Things got worse in 1968, and the unrest burst violently into the open in May. The students revolted against a form of education which was no longer adapted to modern life. Violent clashes took place, and the agitation spread to the whole country. The workers and then the public services went on strike: in a matter of days, the whole country was paralyzed. After a month of uncertainty, de Gaulle and Pompidou took charge of affairs firmly once again. Major social advantages (wage increases) were granted to the workers and to all civil servants. Most Frenchmen had been shocked by the violence. The electors voting for the new Assembly returned a massive Gaullist majority. A law was passed, altering the status of the universities.

De Gaulle then turned again to his project for regionalization and the transformation of the Senate, which he had had to drop during the unrest of 1968. This project, which was to be put to Frenchmen in the form of a referendum, met with stiff opposition from the left, and even from the center-right of Giscard d'Estaing. The project was rejected by a small majority (52%). That same evening, General de Gaulle resigned as President of the Republic. He died 19 months later, in November 1970.

Chronology

52 B.C.	Conquest of Gaul by Julius Caesar. Defeat of Vercingetorix at Alesia. Roman Gaul.
About 275 A.D.	First barbarian invasions in Gaul.
410	The great invasions of Gaul. The first barbarian kingdoms.
451	Attila and the Huns defeated at the Catalaunian fields.
481	Clovis, king of the Franks. Frankish Gaul
496	Victory of Tolbiac. Clovis becomes converted to Catholicism.
639	Death of Dagobert. A series of royal nonentities.
732	Victory of Charles Martel over the Arabs at Poitiers.
771	Charlemagne sole king of the Franks.
800	Charlemagne is crowned Emperor of the West.
843	Treaty of Verdun. The empire is divided into three kingdoms.
987	Hugues Capet and the Capetian dynasty.
1154–1259	War between Capetians and Plantagenets.
1214	Victory of Philippe Auguste at Bouvines.
1328	Philippe VI de Valois.
1337–1475	The Hundred Years' War.
1346	Defeat at Crecy.
1356	Defeat at Poitiers-Maupertuis.
1370–1372	Du Guesclin and Charles V drive out the English.
1415	Defeat at Azincourt. One third of France is occupied.
1429	Joan of Arc. The liberation of Orleans.
1453	France is entirely liberated as a result of French victory at Castillon.
1494	Frist French expeditions in Italy.
1515	Francis I victorious at Marignan.
1559	Treaty of Cateau-Cambresis. End of the Italian wars.
1562–1598	The Wars of Religion in France.
1572	St. Bartholomew's Day massacre.
1589	Assassination of Henry III. Henry IV (of the House of Bourbon) becomes king.
1598	The Edict of Nantes.
1610	Assassination of Henry IV.
1635	France enters the Thirty Years' War.
1648	Treaty of Westphalia.
1659	Treaty of the Pyrenees.
1685	Revocation of the Edict of Nantes.
1713–1714	Treaties of Utrecht and Rastatt.
1745	Louis XV victorious at Fontenoy.
1748	Treaty of Aix-la-Chapelle.
1763	Treaty of Paris. France loses India and Canada.
1774–1789	Economic crisis.
1789	Taking of the Bastille. The Rights of Man.
1792	Collapse of the monarchy. The first Republic.
1793	Execution of Louis XVI. The Terror.
1799	*Coup d'etat* by Napoleon on 18 Brumaire.
1804	Napoleon Bonaparte becomes Emperor.
1805	Victory at Austerlitz.
1812	The restreat from Russia.
1814	Abdication of Napoleon I. Restoration of the Bourbons.
1830	Fall of the Bourbons. Louis-Philippe, king of France.
1848	Fall of Louis Philippe. The Second Republic.
1852–1870	Napoleon III and the Second Empire.
1870	Disaster at Sedan. The Third Republic.
1914	The First World War. Victory on the Marne.
1916	Victory at Verdun.
1918	The Armistice. The Allies triumphant.
1939	The Second World War.
1940	France crushed and occupied. De Gaulle in London.
1944	The Allies land in Normandy. Paris is liberated. The Fourth Republic.
1946–1954	The War in Indo-China.
1954–1962	The War in Algeria.
1958	General de Gaulle comes to power. The Fifth Republic.
1968	Rioting in May throughout France.
1969	Resignation of General de Gaulle.